DIRECT INTERVENTION

DIRECT INTERVENTION
CANADA-FRANCE RELATIONS
1967-1974

ELDON BLACK

CARLETON LIBRARY SERIES
187

Carleton University Press

Canadian Cataloguing in Publication Data

Black, Eldon, date.
    Direct intervention : Canada-France relations,
1967-1974

(Carleton library series ; 187)
Includes bibliographical references and index.
ISBN 0-88629-289-1

    1. Canada—Foreign relations—France.
2. France—Foreign relations—Canada. 3. Canada—
Foreign relations—1945-   . I. Title. II. Series.

FC247.B53 1996   327.71044   C96-900698-5
F1029.5.F8B53 1996

Cover Design: Your Aunt Nellie
Typeset: Mayhew & Associates Graphic Communications, Richmond, Ont.

Carleton University Press gratefully acknowledges the support extended to its
publishing program by the Canada Council and the financial assistance of the
Ontario Arts Council. The Press would also like to thank the Department of
Canadian Heritage, Government of Canada, and the Government of Ontario
through the Ministry of Culture, Tourism and Recreation, for their assistance.

To Francine, my partner in the Foreign Service,
and to my colleagues at the Canadian Embassy Paris.

CONTENTS

ACKNOWLEDGEMENTS ix
PREFACE 1
Prologue: 1960-1967 5
1 Arrival in Paris: General De Gaulle's Press Conference 17
2 Early Days: Some Protagonists 23
3 La Francophonie and the Outbreak of Hostilities:
The Gabon Affair 29
4 The Trials of an Elder Statesman: The Events of May 1968 41
5 A Transatlantic Slanging Match: The Rossillon Affair 47
6 A Premier Dies, Two Prime Ministers Meet 55
7 "Business as Usual" 59
8 An Exchange of Ambassadors 73
9 Jean-Guy Cardinal in Paris: Space Communications 77
10 Hostilities in Africa, Round Two 85
11 De Gaulle Departs, Gaullism Remains 95
12 The New French Government: The Policy of Duality 105
13 A Disastrous Autumn 109
14 Much Ado About Visits 127
15 The Second Niamey Conference: Hostilities in Africa,
Round Three 133
16 First Steps toward Normalization: Mitchell Sharp Visits Paris 143
17 Renewal of the Franco-Canadian Cultural Agreement
and the Quebec Election 149
18 A New Ambassador—The October Crisis—The End
of an Era 157
19 Normalization: Bourassa Visits Paris, Schumann Comes
to Ottawa 167
20 Canada and the European Community: A Canadian
Prime Minister Returns to Paris 179
ENVOI 193
APPENDIX 195
BIBLIOGRAPHY 199
INDEX 201

ILLUSTRATIONS

1 Premier Johnson's funeral   56

2 Two Blackfoot nation dancers   96

3 Canadian Embassy colleagues in Paris   110

4 The opening of the Canadian Cultural Centre   147

5 Presenting Letters of Credence at the Elysée Palace   163

6 Schumann visits Ottawa   177

7 Trudeau meets with Giscard d'Estaing   187

8 The author   190

ACKNOWLEDGEMENTS

I WOULD NOT HAVE PERSEVERED with this book without the encouragement of Ambassador Paul Tremblay and the late The Right Honorable Jean-Luc Pepin who read the first draft. I am grateful to fellow colleagues and authors Peter Roberts and John Starnes for their wise advice. The late Bill Hooper provided friendly and never-failing assistance to a neophyte on a computer. I should also like to thank the following for their help either in tracking down, or permitting me to use, photographs: The Honorable Léo Cadieux, Ian Clark, Guy Plamondon, Tim Creery and Léopold Amyot.

Greg Donaghy of the Historical Section of the Department of Foreign Affairs and International Trade was both cheerful and effective as he guided me through the pitfalls of approval from the Department and the mysteries of the Access to Information Act. I was helped in my research by Ron Falls of the Access to Information Section, National Archives, and Cuineas Boyle, Coordinator of Access to Information at the Privy Council Office.

My copy editor Noel Gates did yeoman work in helping to transform the manuscript into a volume fit for a university press. The team at Carleton University Press, led by John Flood and Jennifer Strickland, guided it through to publication with enterprise and dedication.

PREFACE

THE THREE-SIDED CONFLICT between the governments of Canada, Quebec and France over Quebec's place in Canada and the world has been the subject of much writing and discussion. If this book undertakes to add something to that debate, it is because there has, until now, been little written on the subject by representatives of the federal government and because, during much of the period in question, its author occupied a unique vantage point from which to observe events. This account will not engage in a fresh examination of the views and motives of *indépendantistes* and federalists in Quebec, or of the shaping of Quebec's international policy by its successive governments; nor does it reopen the question of whether General Charles De Gaulle really intended to cry "Vive le Quebec libre!" from the balcony of Montreal's City Hall in July 1967. The General's motives have been made clear with the passage of time, and evidence of them is referred to in the course of this narrative.

This is an account of what happened after De Gaulle's visit, during the period of regular and direct intervention by the French government in Canadian internal affairs. It traces the series of crises and confrontations which eventually led to a modus vivendi, more or less acceptable to all parties. The personal viewpoint is that of a former Minister at the Canadian Embassy in Paris (from 1967 to 1971), and subsequently a senior official in Ottawa, who was directly engaged in Canada's relations with France. This approach attempts to convey what it was like to represent Canada in the capital of a power which had once ruled it as a colony, which had been an ally throughout this present century, and whose president was directly interfering in Canadian domestic affairs.

Describing events in which one personally participated a quarter of a century ago is a task of some difficulty. Judgments must be based, as much as possible, on how one thought and acted at the time, and not modified by what has happened since. Recollections have been verified with the cooperation of the Department of Foreign Affairs and International Trade, formerly the Department of External Affairs, the National

1

Archives of Canada and the Privy Council Office. These organizations have made files available which form the basis for the book, sources supplemented by personal correspondence, discussions with former colleagues and media reports.

Any history is inevitably coloured by its author's own background, and if he holds strong views, based on his own experience and upbringing, he owes it to his readers to explain what they are and from whence they derive. What follows is a summary of my own cultural and linguistic origins.

I am what used to be called an "English-speaking Canadian," born, raised and educated in Montreal. I went to private schools where I was taught French grammar without ever speaking the language, and I lived in a community where the only French heard was in the kitchen or on the farm. During World War II, when I joined the Navy, I was first posted to Trois-Rivières and Quebec City, and began to realize that I had been living within a society whose language and culture I did not know. Summers on the Lower St. Lawrence and in Paris, a fascination with Quebec politics, my years at the McGill Law Faculty and, most important of all, my marriage to someone whose mother tongue was French, wrought many changes in my personality and my opinions. My wife was Belgo-Luxembourgeoise, for whom English was her fifth language. She did not view culture or her mother tongue from the standpoint of a minority, and the French language and culture became part of our life together and of the lives of our children.

The Quebec in which I found myself living at the completion of my law studies in 1949 was one in which the French-speaking majority was mired in Premier Maurice Duplessis' narrow provincialism and strongly influenced by the Roman Catholic Church as it was before Vatican II. As for the English-speaking minority, much of it enjoyed an inward and self-satisfied life of its own. I strongly believed then, and still do, that Canada's future as a country required French Canada to play a full or even a leading part in the life of the country as a whole, instead of erecting walls between the two linguistic communities. I also believed that the "French Fact" in our national life had to be encouraged if we were to build a different kind of country from the colossus to the south. None of this seemed likely to occur in 1949 and I considered myself fortunate to be able to leave the introspection of Montreal and occupy myself with the more serious problems of the postwar world by entering the Department of External Affairs. My mood on leaving Montreal was best expressed in the words of a Governor General, the Earl Grey, who wrote to King Edward VII in 1905, "The English people of Montreal would be much gayer and happier and more cultured if they allowed a little French sunlight to warm and illuminate their lives."

My early years in the Foreign Service were shaped by my first posting to Stalin's Moscow, and I worked for many years in the areas of defence policy and foreign intelligence. In 1965 I was posted to Belgium and had an opportunity to witness at first hand the tribal, linguistic and cultural disputes in which the Walloons and the Flemings have engaged throughout the centuries.

Events in Canada were now to change my career decisively. Governor General Georges-Philéas Vanier died and Prime Minister Pearson replaced him with Roland Michener, the High Commissioner to India. The minister in the embassy in Paris was sent to India and there was a vacancy in Paris, in the position that is occupied by the Ambassador's deputy.

It is a tradition in the Foreign Service that whenever possible, High Commisioners who represent Canada in London should have English as their mother tongue, and deputies should be French-speaking, while their counterparts in Paris, the Ambassadors, should speak French as their mother tongue and be supported by English-speaking Ministers. In External Affairs in 1967, there were few adequately bilingual English-speaking Canadians at the appropriate level, and suddenly I found myself asked to go to Paris to be looked over by Jules Léger, the Ambassador. We got on well, partly, I like to think, because I told him my views on the place of French Canada within the country as a whole.

I was to go to Paris forthwith and had to leave my wife and four children in Brussels until the Christmas break. We were fortunate with our accommodation: General de Gaulle had just done us a great personal favour by removing France from the North Atlantic Treaty Organization [NATO] Integrated Command and requiring all NATO personnel to leave France. In consequence, we inherited the large and comfortable apartment which had been occupied by Canada's NATO ambassador. It was an ideal place for our complex family of four children, ranging in age from an eldest daughter of 16, partly in a wheel chair and partly on crutches, to the youngest, a boy of two. It was to prove a haven during the difficult years that lay ahead.

PROLOGUE: 1960-1967

FROM THE END OF WORLD WAR II relations between Canada and France had been good but not particularly close. Though we were allies in NATO, France was preoccupied by economic recovery, European security, the Common Market and decolonization. Quebec attitudes under Duplessis remained isolationist, while Canada followed a policy of close alliance with the U.S., dictated by considerations of trade and security from the Soviet Union, and into which the French character of Quebec rarely entered as a factor. Canada's main international interests were multilateral and were channelled through the United Nations, NATO and the evolving Commonwealth.

This situation was to change dramatically in 1960. France was once again ruled by General De Gaulle, recalled to save the Republic and save Algeria for France, but forced to give Algeria its independence and to commence the dissolution of the French empire. In Quebec the "Quiet Revolution" steered by Premier Jean Lesage's Liberals started a series of massive changes designed to bring the province into the twentieth century. Two of these changes are particularly relevant to the present narrative: the replacement of the Catholic Church by the State as the body directing education in French-language schools, and the manifestation by the French-speaking majority of a growing interest in the outside world. The new Quebec rediscovered France, the former mother country, but it also discovered a wider Francophone world, once part of the French or Belgian Empires, consisting of some twenty-five countries, situated largely in West Africa, where the language and culture of the ruling elites was French.

In the early 1960s an increasing series of visits took place between Quebec and France, and a particular relationship was established. Quebec sought France's aid for the modernization of its educational system and for the protection of its language and culture. In Ottawa the federal government, under the leadership of Prime Minister John Diefenbaker, did not react to the moves made by Quebec, nor did it appear to understand that action by one province in the international sphere might represent a danger to national unity. In 1963 the Pearson government came into power, and at an early date it appointed the Royal Commission on Bilingualism and Biculturalism to undertake a detailed study of all aspects of the relationship between English and French Canada. At the same time it engaged in a program of cooperative federalism which was directed particularly toward Quebec. It also proposed programs within the federal sphere of competence to protect the language and culture of French-speaking Canadians living outside Quebec, numbering about one million. For the successful implementation of these new departures in policy, Canada needed a closer relationship with France.

In the meantime, cooperation between Quebec and France was progressing. By 1964 Quebec was already close to completing an agreement with France on education, and it was negotiating wider agreements in the areas of culture, technical cooperation and youth exchanges. Ottawa needed to make up for past inaction, especially if it wished to preserve federal responsibility for relations with foreign countries and prevent Quebec from establishing an independent international personality separate from that of Canada. The federal government opened consulates in Bordeaux and Marseilles (both since closed), it negotiated cultural agreements with the partially French-speaking countries of Belgium and Switzerland, and in 1965 it signed a Master Agreement [Accord-Cadre] on cultural cooperation with France just before Quebec signed a similar agreement. This agreement permitted Quebec and the other provinces, if they so wished, to have particular agreements with France, provided they were applied to areas of exclusive provincial jurisdiction such as education, and that Ottawa was consulted and concurred.

De Gaulle's attitude to Canada and Quebec had been and would continue to be a function of France's interests as he saw them at a given time. During the war he needed Canada's help and a quotation from his speech to the Canadian Parliament in 1944 sets the tone: "France is sure of finding at her side, and in agreement with her, the people who know her well. That is to say, she is sure of finding Canada first of all." [1] Of his return in 1960, in the middle of the Diefenbaker era and some months before the election of the Lesage government in Quebec, he wrote in 1970 that he found a situation that had been covered over by the War, namely "a state perpetually incompatible, ambiguous and artificial." [2] When he left, he thought that Canada would find its future in "two cooperating states, one of French and one of British origin, preferably associating their independencies in order to better remain Canadian."[3] This statement, notable for its ambiguity, resembles the sovereignty-association theory. The reader may wish to decide whether the General himself developed it at that time or whether he was persuaded of its validity by some of his Quebec visitors during the 1960s.

Quebec's agreement with France on the subject of education was signed in 1965. In the preceding years, visits of Quebec ministers to Paris had multiplied: Premier Lesage himself was received three times by De Gaulle between 1961 and 1965. During this period of cooperative federalism the Pearson government did not object to such visits, provided it was kept informed and the matters under discussion were within provincial jurisdiction. As the relationship with France grew closer, two views developed in Quebec on the best way to use it to the province's own advantage. There were those, mostly politicians, who saw it as a tool to pry further powers from Ottawa in the domestic and international fields. There was another group, initially consisting mostly of civil servants led by Claude Morin, the most influential constitutional adviser and at that time Chairman of the Interdepartmental Commission on External Affairs, who saw it as a way to establish Quebec's international personality and eventually achieve separation.

The 1965 Education Agreement was the first of its kind. Before its signature, Morin set out the options for the Quebec Minister Paul Gérin-Lajoie, noting that "on international agreements Quebec should be able to sign in areas of concurrent jurisdiction on its own though in consultation with Ottawa as and when necessary." Morin said further that the ultimate objective should be an amendment to the constitution giving Quebec a limited international competence in specified areas. On the conclusion of the Education Agreement the Quebec government asserted that it did not need Ottawa's permission to conclude international agreements in its own areas of jurisdiction. A year later, in advice to the new Premier Daniel Johnson, Morin stated that "only a constitutional evolution toward a Confederation of States would permit Quebec to acquire a complete international personality allowing it to conclude agreements with foreign countries, have diplomatic and consular representatives abroad and pass laws with extra-territorial consequences."[4]

Premier Johnson, more nationalist than Lesage and aware of the rising threat from the separatist movement, saw Morin's approach as a useful lever to employ against Ottawa in forthcoming constitutional talks. It was not surprising therefore that, during Johnson's visit to De Gaulle in 1966, negotiations between France and Quebec were announced in areas where the federal government also had jurisdiction, such as communications by satellite.

The Pearson government also wished to have France's cooperative assistance for its own policies of bilingualism and biculturalism. Pearson visited De Gaulle in January 1964 and was well received. The General said all the right things: "France had no intention of creating difficulties for Canada or of interfering in its national affairs. He regarded Canadians of French origin with special affection and was particularly interested in their development and progress but he did not intend to let the closeness of these ties hinder relations between France and the Federal Government."[5]

Throughout the talks, however, it was clear that De Gaulle took it for granted that Canadian reactions were always influenced by Washington, which made dialogue difficult, since De Gaulle's policy was strongly anti-American. He viewed Canada through the prism of France's own continental history, the ancient rivalry with the British and the new threat from an all-embracing English-speaking world created by British decolonization and the rise of U.S. power.

At the time these talks took place De Gaulle was playing a double game. He saw his help to the "French of North America," as he called French-speaking Canadians, as part of his policy of grandeur for France as a world power. Such a France had obligations to those she had abandoned two hundred years previously. Someone of his generation could not conceive of an international order that was not founded on the sovereign nation state, defined ethnically, for this concept was deeply rooted in the history of France. Federations and multinational societies were beyond his experience. Quebec's future was to be that of a nation state, with vague unspecified economic and defence relations with the rest of Canada—the Austro-Hungarian solution, as the General liked to call it. So that the same year in which he was assuring Prime Minister Pearson that he did not intend to interfere in Canadian affairs, he was telling Premier Lesage that "all that was happening in Quebec was bound to end in some form of independence."[6]

Meanwhile, Ottawa tried to continue the dialogue with the General. Pearson wrote a letter in March 1966 reminding De Gaulle of the '64 meeting, which was the start of a *resserrement* ("tightening") of relations between the two countries. The Prime Minister noted that progress had been made in the cultural and academic fields, and to a considerably lesser extent in trade relations, and that there had been regular consultations between the Canadian Secretary of State for External Affairs and the French Foreign Minister. The General replied the following month, agreeing that since 1964 Franco-Canadian relations had progressed in a harmonious manner in the common interest of both countries. To those suspicious of De Gaulle's motives this letter had troublesome overtones. It was dated two days after the General had announced France's withdrawal from the NATO integrated command and requested her allies, including Canada, to remove their troops and military bases from French soil, a move which, inevitably, led to a strong protest and a demand for compensation on the part of Canada. The General's letter ended with the following ambiguous phrase: "His participation at the World Exhibition in Montreal, should, he hopes, testify in an eloquent fashion to the value France attaches to reinforcing Franco-Canadian links."[7]

And of course, in July 1967 De Gaulle did come to Canada. He made his speeches in Quebec, was enthusiastically received on the Chemin du Roy, shouted "Vive le Quebec libre" in Montreal and, on learning of the reaction of the Canadian government, returned to Paris without going to Ottawa.

English Canada had taken nearly a century to grow away from its neo-colonial ties with the United Kingdom, and now Canada's other former colonial power had made an explosive reappearance on the scene. This introduction of a third outside party was to unduly complicate and often falsify the debate on national unity that was currently proceeding in Canada, and to make extremely difficult the task of those Canadians who believed that Canada only made sense as a country if the linguistic rights and culture of French Canada were protected, and that all French-speaking Canadians had the opportunity to play a full role in national life.

The minutes of the two Cabinet meetings called on July 25, 1967 to discuss De Gaulle's behaviour in Quebec[8] show clearly that the ministers realized they faced a major crisis in relations between the two founding peoples. All possibilities were considered, ranging from maintenance of the original program, which would bring De Gaulle to Ottawa and would permit a confrontation with him, to a request that he return home immediately. Under Pearson's leadership a consensus was reached: it was recognized that there had to be a response to the General's actions—the country demanded no less. There would be a positive acknowledgment of the welcome that De Gaulle had received from the people of Quebec, a rejection of the encouragement he had given to separatism and, at the same time, a restatement of Canada's intention of maintaining friendship with

France. The message would leave the way open for the General's visit to Ottawa, so that if he refused, it would clearly be his own decision.

There was another aspect of De Gaulle's public statements that was particularly unacceptable, especially for Canadians of both languages who had fought on French soil in two World Wars: he compared his reception by the crowds in Quebec with events surrounding the liberation of Paris from German occupation in 1944. He seemed to equate the situation of French-speaking Canadians with that of the French people under the Nazis. Hence the statement by the Canadian government in its reply to De Gaulle that "Canadians are free. Every province is free. Canadians do not need to be liberated."[9]

The contributions of two future prime ministers to the Cabinet's discussion are worth recording. The new Minister of Justice, Pierre Trudeau, said people in France would think the Canadian government was weak if it did not react; the General did not have the support of the intellectuals in his own country and the French press was opposed to him. A young Minister without portfolio named Jean Chrétien expressed similar views. He informed his colleagues that the government of Quebec had chartered buses to transport people from his constituency to Trois-Rivières for organized demonstrations during the General's passage. He was of the view that the government should show no weakness. Months later, at the Embassy in Paris, we were visited by a group of Union Nationale organizers who were still congratulating themselves on how well their political machine had managed the transfer of people to cheer De Gaulle.

On August 24, De Gaulle called a meeting of his Council of Ministers [Cabinet], an unheard of event in the season when the whole of France is on vacation. A decision was taken to considerably increase France's assistance to Quebec in cultural, economic and technical areas. On September 10, the French Minister of Education, Alain Peyrefitte, arrived in Quebec to sign a series of agreements, and was followed shortly after by François Missoffe, Minister of Sport and Youth, to start negotiations for an Office of Quebec-France Youth Exchanges, a subject not included in the Accord-Cadre between Canada and France. The French Ministers went straight to Quebec and Ottawa was neither informed of their arrival nor of the outcome of their visits.

France was now dealing directly with Quebec without informing the federal government, and Ottawa had to face the prospect that, if this process continued, it would lose control both in form and in fact over an aspect of Canadian foreign policy and create precedents for the future, not only for Quebec but for the other provinces as well. For this reason, definition of the conditions under which French ministers and officials would visit Quebec became one of the major issues between the two countries.

A group of officials at External Affairs, which was chaired by the Undersecretary, Marcel Cadieux, and included Ambassador Léger, met in August to prepare an analysis of the General's visit and recommendations for future action. Their findings were passed to the Prime Minister, and were to constitute the basis of Ottawa's policy toward France and Quebec in the years that followed.[10]

The group detected four main themes underlying the General's behaviour. The first was his anti-Americanism. He believed that U.S. global power continued to be the main threat to France and the French language and culture, and he had appealed to Quebec to join France in preserving that language and culture against American pressure. He implied by omission that he did not expect English-speaking Canada to share these aims, or to have the will to resist pressure from the U.S. The second theme was "national liberation." De Gaulle apparently associated the Quiet Revolution in Quebec with the movement for emancipation from colonial rule elsewhere in the world, which he had recently confronted in the French empire. He thus revealed his conviction that independence for Quebec was inevitable. He also left the impression that he believed the Quebec government of the day shared his conviction.

The third theme was solidarity with Quebec. De Gaulle regarded the Quebec government as the government of all French Canadians. France would provide the help Quebec required and he implied this would be done without reference to Ottawa. Finally there was the theme of moral necessity. The General believed that he had to go to the heart of things during his visit to Canada, regardless of international practice; France had to help French Canadians because of their origins. French Canada was not a country and therefore the principle of non-interference did not apply, particularly as the Quebec government had requested and approved France's intention to provide assistance.

De Gaulle appeared to be solely responsible for the cast he had given to his Canadian trip; clearly his officials had been taken by surprise. The public and press reaction in France ranged from puzzlement to outright disagreement. For many French people the performance in Canada, when taken with other examples of De Gaulle's erratic behaviour, was yet another example of their leader's decline.

By appealing to French Canadian pride in their origins and their determination to affirm their identity, the General had struck a responsive chord and released a good deal of pent-up emotion and resentment. This reaction, however, did not necessarily amount to support for independence. Mayor Jean Drapeau of Montreal probably expressed the views of the majority when he reaffirmed Quebec's determination to preserve its French heritage and develop relations with France, but at the same time to retain its identity within Canada and to reject any dependent relationship with France. The Johnson government had certainly expected to gain political capital from its policy of special status for Quebec, but was not prepared for the General's outburst prophesying an independent Quebec.

For Canada as a whole, the differences between the reactions of the English-speaking and French-speaking populations were clearly marked. English-speaking Canadians laid emphasis on national unity and expressed resentment at the General's encouragement to the separatist movement in Quebec. In French Canada, where the emphasis was on changing the status quo, the dominant reaction was satisfaction that the need to preserve and strengthen the French Fact in Canada had been underlined. While the visit brought out the ever present differences within the country, it also revealed basic agreement that Canada's problems must be solved by Canadians, and that despite De Gaulle, close relations with France were in the interests of Canada as a whole.

The group of officials concluded that:

As long as De Gaulle remained in power Ottawa would have to realize that there would be recurring crises that would inevitably affect any progress in Franco-Canadian relations. Nevertheless, Ottawa should stick to its policy of a balance between rejection of outside interference and reaffirmation of the importance it attached to relations with France. Canada should, difficult though it might be, try to maintain an attitude of 'business as usual,' at least until De Gaulle, by further actions, required us to take more active measures against either France or Quebec or both. In the end it was in Canada, not in France, that the fate of Confederation would be decided. The inescapable conclusion was that Ottawa and Quebec must have a continuing dialogue. Whether common ground could be found was another question, but it was essential that Ottawa make the effort.

In September the French government announced the creation of a new inter-governmental organization by France and Quebec, to be chaired on the French side by the Secretary of State for Foreign Affairs, the minister second highest in rank at the French Foreign Ministry. The organization was to function on the basis of equality between the two sides, and in addition to its meetings there would be "organic" meetings between the respective ministers responsible for economic affairs and education, to further common action in these areas. Furthermore, meetings at the highest level involving all interested ministers would take place regularly in Quebec and Paris. Separate talks were also reported on a joint Quebec-France venture in satellite communications, which would be a follow-up to discussions during Premier Johnson's visit in 1966.

It is difficult to understand why Premier Johnson, a politician to his fingertips, agreed to such an all-embracing agreement. It would not be highly popular in Quebec, where many disliked the "French of France," and it would not improve relations with other provinces in the forthcoming constitutional talks. In retrospect, his action may best be viewed as that of a man in a hurry, who knew he had a heart condition. The Embassy in Paris soon learnt that he was planning to visit Paris again within the next few months. At about this time the wits of Paris began to describe him as the "Sous-Préfet du Québec" and in fact, a tendency did become discernible for French officials to patronize Quebec in the same manner as the recently created independent states of the former French empire.

De Gaulle and Quebec had substantially raised the stakes in the transatlantic diplomatic game and, quite naturally, there was a strong reaction in Ottawa. The question of satellite communications was quickly dealt with: a statement was made in the House of Commons that communications was a field falling exclusively within federal jurisdiction. The experts in Canada and France knew this already, for they had previously exchanged experience and would continue to do so. The satellite chosen by France and Quebec, which was named "Symphonie," was not particularly attractive, since it would only be a test vehicle and was already incorporated into an existing Franco-German program.

The new consultation machinery represented a more serious problem. There was no mention of it in previous agreements between Quebec and France. Regular consultation was new, as was economic cooperation. Ottawa took the view that the latest French action amounted to a recognition of a measure of sovereignty for Quebec in the international sphere. There had been no consultation with, much less mention of, the federal government and, as stated above, the new organization was to function between France and Quebec, with their ministers treated as being of equal standing.

Prime Minister Pearson took the advice of his officials that, in the first instance, Ottawa should react cautiously and ask the French for clarification of the significance of their activities, how they reconciled them with the agreements already existing between the two countries, and the requirements of international law and courtesy.[11] These questions were really unanswerable, but Ottawa hoped that posing them would encourage those at the Quai D'Orsay who had helped to calm troubled waters in the past to do so again, provided they did not consider that the matter had to be raised with the General. Léger was sent instructions to see Hervé Alphand, the Secretary General of the Foreign Ministry, while the French Ambassador was called in by Undersecretary Cadieux. The French sent a message which could be construed as a reply and which indicated that they had been engaged in some damage control. Léger was informed by Alphand that the French government agreed to keep the Canadian government informed of any visits by French ministers to Quebec, and it was not excluded that French ministers might visit Ottawa; in fact, none did until after De Gaulle's departure from the scene.

Ottawa was partially satisfied but instructed Léger to ask that it be informed in advance of the program and purposes of these visits so that it could decide, when appropriate, to ask a visiting French minister to Ottawa. The visits question was much in the press, so Paul Martin, the Secretary of State for External Affairs, stated in the Commons that French ministers were always welcome to visit Canada. Unfortunately, he added that relations with France were normal. They were not. At this point a serious disagreement became evident between Ambassador Léger and Undersecretary Cadieux regarding the real nature of those relations and the tactics required to handle them.

Léger had described his latest instructions as "legalisms," an allusion to Marcel Cadieux's previous position as Legal Advisor in the Department of External Affairs. These two men saw the situation very differently. Léger argued that while Canada should not allow any precedent permitting France to help Quebec acquire an international personality, neither should it push the legal approach too far, now that the French Foreign Office was showing some willingness to meet Canada's requirements. Too much emphasis on legal aspects would bring De Gaulle once more into action. Furthermore, there had not necessarily been a deterioration in relations with France; so far as Quebec was concerned there had, in fact, been a great improvement, and now it remained for Ottawa to persuade the French to apply similar policies to all of Canada, particularly to French-speaking Canadians outside Quebec.[12]

When Cadieux read the Embassy telegram expressing these views he added a notation: "Léger will never understand the constitutional and political implications of the new relationship between Quebec and France." He pointed out to Paul Martin that French policy had introduced an outside third party into a Canadian debate and had placed Quebec in a unique position with respect to the rest of Canada. France was, in effect, acting against the federal government's policy of promoting national unity.

That these two men should clash was not surprising. They were friends; they were also rivals, and their origins were very different. Both had served Canada with devotion and distinction, and no two French-speaking Canadians of their generation had done more to improve the atmosphere in which Canadians who shared their mother tongue could work in Ottawa, particularly in the Department of External Affairs. Both had been Undersecretary, Léger in the heady days of Prime Minister Louis Saint-Laurent, Pearson and the Suez crisis, when there were no serious federal-provincial problems in the international area, Cadieux in the 1960s, when the Quiet Revolution and Quebec's drive for an international personality created day-to-day concerns about Canada's constitutional future.

They were very different in character and had had quite different experiences of France. Cadieux was a tough city boy and a distinguished international lawyer, somewhat authoritarian, demanding excellence from his French-speaking officers who, representing a minority, had to show that the French Fact was an advantage and a necessity for the Canadian Foreign Service. He was suspicious of France's motives. He had seen the patronizing way the French had treated the French-speaking Walloons in Belgium after the Second World War and, as a member of one of the first Indo-China International Commissions, he had seen the legacy of French imperial policy.

Léger came from the countryside, a tall reflective man with a wide culture and considerable personal charm. He had worked as a reporter in Ottawa and received a French government scholarship to complete his studies in France, where he met and married his delightful and witty wife, Gaby. For him France held many happy memories, which made the difficulties of his posting to Paris all the harder to bear. To a Foreign Service Officer who is posted abroad, the first priority is the maintenance of a sound relationship with the country to which he is accredited, whereas service in Ottawa means exposure to the daily political pressures of concern to the government in office. When the crisis over Quebec was evolving, Léger had been out of Canada for ten years.

Cadieux obtained Martin's approval to go to Paris and argue out the policy differences with Léger directly. Their discussion, which was tense, was summarized by Cadieux in a memorandum to the Minister dated November 11, 1967 which appears in the Appendix to this volume. As this document shows, agreement was eventually reached, and Cadieux's summary sets out very clearly the problems faced by the Embassy and by the government in Ottawa in their attempt to counter French interventionist policies.

Léger saw Alphand on November 23 and placed his instructions in the context of a desire on Canada's part not to reduce the new cooperation between Quebec and France, but rather to broaden this policy to include all of Canada. The reply came four days later at a press conference given by De Gaulle: the General announced in public, for the first time, his belief in, and support for, an independent Quebec.

NOTES

1. De Gaulle, *War Memoirs: Unity 1944-1946*, 246.
2. De Gaulle, *Mémoires d'espoir: Le Renouveau, 1958-1963*, 251.
3. *Ibid.*, 255
4. Documents received under the Access to Information Act, Ref. 1025-9-92170.
5. Memorandum to Prime Minister Pearson from Secretary of State for External Affairs Paul Martin, January 11, 1967.
6. Dale Thomson, *Vive le Québec libre*, 137.
7. External Affairs, File 20-1-2-Fr. vol. 4
8. Cabinet Minutes, no. 87050 20-1-9, July 25, 1967.
9. *Mike: Memoirs Lester B. Pearson*, vol. 3, 268
10. Memorandum to Prime Minister Pearson, from Secretary of State for Extrenal Affairs Paul Martin, September 6, 1967.
11. Memorandum to Prime Minister Pearson, from Secretary of State for External Affairs Paul Martin, September 22, 1967.
12. Embassy Paris Telegram to Ottawa, no. 3114, October 13, 1967.

1

ARRIVAL IN PARIS
GENERAL DE GAULLE'S PRESS CONFERENCE

MY TOUR OF DUTY in Paris began on the morning of November 27, 1967 the day that De Gaulle stated his public position on the status of Quebec. When I was greeted by my new Ambassador, Jules Léger, he suggested that in order to appreciate the atmosphere in which I would have to work, I should attend the press conference to be given by De Gaulle that afternoon, at which he was expected to amplify his views on Quebec and Canada.

Press conferences by the General had over the years become a ritual set piece. They provided a stage on which he could use his undoubted talents as an actor, orator and prophet to pronounce on French foreign and domestic policy and offer his interpretation of international events of the day.

The conferences took place in the main reception Salon of the Elysée Palace. The audience was a mixture of foreign diplomats, senior French bureaucrats and the French and international press, while the General was surrounded by the members of his Cabinet. This was the sixteenth performance since his return to power in 1958. The questions had as usual been arranged in advance, and the chosen reporter for the Quebec question was the correspondent of Montreal's *La Presse*, an assiduous indépendantiste. After the conference was over I returned to the Embassy, and the following account is from the message I sent to Ottawa that evening.[1]

The General started with a Gaullist history of the French-speaking peoples of Canada, "a country discovered, populated and administered by the French." He then described the immigration from Britain and other parts of Europe to English-speaking Canada, "which together with the U.S., had tried to seduce the French into renouncing their own heritage. By a miracle a nation has survived in Quebec and remains as French as ever. However, recently it has realized that passive defence is not enough and wishes to become master of its own destiny, particularly in the cultural and economic areas. Quebec looks to France for help and the mother country is willing to give considerable assistance."

With regard to his exclamation "Vive le Québec libre," the General said "that whether Quebec would be free was the central question and this would have to be resolved with the rest of Canada. For him two conditions were necessary: first a complete change in the Canadian constitution which would eventually lead to the creation of a sovereign Quebec; and secondly, solidarity of the French communities on both sides of the Atlantic, including the French communities outside Quebec. The next meeting of the French and Quebec governments would give impetus to this solidarity." What this last point meant was never clear, though we knew that the General wanted a meeting with Premier Johnson, which the latter postponed because of the forthcoming constitutional negotiations in Toronto.

With this speech De Gaulle clearly prophesied an independent Quebec, a goal which he supported, but meanwhile Canada had to determine what were to be the day-to-day relations between Gaullist France and the federal government, the Quebec government and those provincial governments which had important French-speaking minorities.

As a final footnote to this episode the General concluded his remarks on Canada with a resounding quotation from the French poet Paul Valéry, and wondered how he would have viewed De Gaulle's visit to Canada. The following morning, the Canadian Ambassador to the United Nations Economic, Social and Cultural Organization [UNESCO] received an indignant visit from his French opposite number, who was Valéry's son, to inform him that the General had misquoted his father.

While the General was giving his press conference, Pearson was returning from delivering a speech in London, so that the first reaction in Ottawa, given by Paul Martin, had to be provisional pending a meeting of the full Cabinet. The constitutional talks on "Confederation of Tomorrow" had taken place in Toronto with Premier Johnson in attendance. He had said in his opening statement that first of all "we are all Canadians" and then proceeded to outline Quebec's desires for a form of "special status." The General's press conference seems to have come as a complete surprise to him and he avoided any official response. This is an example of how interference by an outside party was beginning to complicate constitutional evolution in Canada.

The federal Cabinet met in the morning and afternoon of November 28, after reading De Gaulle's text.[2] The Prime Minister observed, "that it was now a clear case of intervention by a foreign country in Canada's domestic affairs and resolved once and for all any question of the French President's attitude after his visit in July. The General's remarks came at a time when the English-French dialogue was very active and by distorting facts and emphasizing others the French President was trying to stir up trouble between the two founding peoples." Paul Martin said that the General's remarks were clearly a long-term policy and that the warnings of some officials over the last three years, particularly the Undersecretary of State for External Affairs (Marcel Cadieux) had been vindicated. All agreed that the crucial front was Quebec, but when there was some suggestion that Premier Johnson might need some help, the Minister of Health and Immigration, Jean Marchand would have none of it: "The Government of Quebec was buying time; it was oriented toward separatism, a position which had not been approved at the last election and which the people of Quebec had never endorsed for the Union Nationale or any other party."

It was accepted by all that some sort of rejection was required and the consensus was that the best method would be, subject to agreement by the Leader of the Opposition, to make a statement in the House of Commons when motions were called. This would permit statements by the leaders of all parties without a potentially divisive debate. At this point the Prime Minister left the room to speak to Robert Stanfield, the Leader of the Opposition, and while he was absent the Minister of Justice, Trudeau, treated his colleagues to a strong attack on government policy. While he agreed with the line to be taken in this instance, "the Government's whole approach to the present constitutional difficulty is pragmatic and incoherent. The Government is forever reacting to isolated incidents and has no overall strategy.... It is not giving leadership to the country ... MPs and local political leaders cannot be expected to take strong positions if the more important national leaders will not stand up to be counted." It was Trudeau's opinion at the time that the Pearson government had been too weak and accommodating to both Quebec and France. He would soon have the opportunity to put his own stamp on this policy: Pearson, who had already decided to resign, announced his intention to do so some two weeks later.[3]

The Prime Minister made his statement on De Gaulle's press conference in the House of Commons in accordance with the discussion in Cabinet,[4] and the other leaders made their own statements. Robert Stanfield said, *inter alia*, "I hope Canadians are mature enough not to allow such interference by somebody outside Canada to affect the relationship among Canadians inside Canada."[5] My favourite statement was that of Caouette of the Créditistes, who observed that "Quebec had more sovereignty within the Canadian Confederation than any country connected with France has ever obtained since France exists [sic]."[6]

The reactions of Ambassador Léger were to the effect that the General's explanations of what he had said in Montreal constituted further interference in Canadian affairs; his declarations had become more unacceptable and the government had to decide whether to reject them once again or to raise the stakes, bearing in mind that it was Canadian policy to maintain good relations with France and that De Gaulle was a temporary phenomenon. He suggested that, before the government took any definitive decision, it should instruct him to seek an explanation of the more litigious aspects of De Gaulle's remarks and, depending on the result, Martin could continue the dialogue with the French Foreign Minister in a few weeks time, at the forthcoming NATO meeting.[7]

Paul Martin then gave his advice to Pearson. After outlining some of the activist options for Canada, such as breaking off relations or recalling the Ambassador, and the likely reactions in Quebec and France, Martin came to the conclusion that as far as possible we should continue our policy of "business as usual," because in effect we had no alternative. This did not mean Canada could do nothing to contain De Gaulle but rather that we should go to the source of the problem, which was in Quebec, not Paris.[8] Pearson agreed with this advice, and wrote to the Premier of Quebec on December 1. He also insisted that we take diplomatic notice of De Gaulle's statement, perhaps by a note asking for an explanation ... and expressing our surprise and regret at this interference in our domestic affairs.[9]

The next event was the meeting between Paul Martin and the French Foreign Minister, Couve de Murville, at the annual NATO meeting in Brussels. Martin reported that he had forty minutes alone with Couve, who was on the defensive, embarassed by the General's press conference, and who left the impression he would do what he could to minimize further repercussions on our relations. Martin did not press Couve unduly, for these were two men who knew that the problem they faced was beyond their control and that the best they could do was to maintain some continuity in relations between Canada and France. Martin had a rogue elephant, the Quebec government, over which Ottawa had little influence at that time, while Couve had an uncontrollable master, De Gaulle, to whom he was completely loyal.

Martin described to Couve the latest constitutional developments in Canada and said that the majority of Canadians had no intention of splitting the country up. Couve replied that France did not want an independent Quebec, General De Gaulle had spoken of sovereignty, "a concept already in your constitution," and not of independence. Martin did not think that Couve believed in his own explanation, but declared: "You have no right to talk about our domestic affairs." [10]

As suggested by Pearson, a piece of paper was left with Couve setting out our various points of difference. Couve was relatively forthcoming about visits and keeping any agreements with Quebec within already existing arrangements between France and Canada but, as he said, he could not always intervene, for these questions were decided elsewhere. Martin's conclusions from the meeting were that within the limits of his position, Canada could count on reasonable cooperation from Couve; the piece of paper might have some deterrent effect, and in any case we should maintain this form of firm but steady pressure. There might be some limited improvement in our relations, but only until De Gaulle had another opportunity of making a gesture, for example, during the expected visit of Premier Johnson.

NOTES

1. Embassy Paris Telegram to Ottawa, no. 3623, November 27, 1967.
2. Cabinet Minutes, nos. 8850 75-3, 8850 75-8, November 28, 1967.
3. *Mike*, vol. 3, 310.
4. House of Commons, *Debates*, 4774, November 28, 1967.
5. *Ibid.*, 4774, November 28, 1967.
6. *Ibid.*, 4776, November 28, 1967.
7. Embassy Paris Telegram to Ottawa, no. 3627, November 28, 1967.
8. Memorandum to Prime Minister Pearson, from Secretary of State for External Affairs Paul Martin, November 29, 1967.
9. Office of the Prime Minister, December 5, 1967.
10. NATO Delegation Telegram to Ottawa, no. 2861, December 13, 1967.

2

EARLY DAYS
SOME PROTAGONISTS

THE FIRST WEEKS of my new posting were spent in visits to the many officers who made up the Embassy, other Canadian agencies in the city, certain
diplomatic colleagues and key contacts at the Quai d'Orsay, the French
Foreign Ministry. Before all this, however, came a call on the head of a
Canadian organization that was not part of the Embassy and not working
for the federal government but which, during the next few years, exercised
considerable influence behind the scenes. This was the Delegation of
Quebec.

The Delegate General greeted me with all the friendly condescension
due to someone who had joined the Department of External Affairs twelve
years after himself. Jean Chapdelaine had been a Canadian Ambassador in
a number of posts and an Assistant Undersecretary of State for External
Affairs in Ottawa. He had hoped to be nominated as Ambassador in Paris,
but when his friend Jules Léger was appointed instead he used his contacts with the Lesage government to be posted to Paris in any case, as
Delegate General of Quebec.

There is little doubt that his experience was useful to successive
Quebec governments,[1] for he served in Paris for twelve years under three
separate administrations before returning to Quebec as diplomatic adviser
to the Parti Québécois government of René Lévesque. Chapdelaine was,
at the time of our meeting, in a unique position. Thanks to De Gaulle's
policies, he had access to the Elysée Palace and the Quai d'Orsay, while
the Canadian Ambassador had only the most formal relationship with the
General, and the Embassy's relations with the Quai were coldly correct.

This fellow-Canadian and his staff, and we at the Embassy, were
placed in a position of continual rivalry, for each represented a government that had an entirely different view of the future of Canada. The
French government, for its part, had espoused the Quebec cause and
had injected itself into Canadian domestic affairs and constitutional

development. Members of the Embassy and the Delegation would see each other regularly at social functions and, of course, try to learn what the other side was doing, but at the same time the fiction was maintained that relations were "normal." It was unacceptable in Canadian political terms that there should be signs of disagreement between us, which would provide the kind of story a hovering Canadian press corps was looking for, so all the courtesies were usually observed on both sides.

My first visit to the Quai d'Orsay was to the man who was to be my main interlocutor and opponent during my posting, Jean-Daniel Jurgensen, Director of the North American Department. Jurgensen was a bulky redhead of remote Danish extraction, who was a fervent, some said fanatic, exponent of Gaullist nationalism with its ethnocentric principles. He was also an extremely competent foreign service officer, and our relations were always strictly professional.

His position, as the officer responsible for relations with Canada and the United States and later as Assistant Political Director, made him one of the most influential of a small group of politicians and bureaucrats who came to be known in the press as the Quebec Mafia. As young men, many had been members of "*Patrie et Progrès*," an organization established by Michel Debré (one of De Gaulle's chief "barons" and his first Prime Minister when he returned to power), to keep alive the flame of a nationalist and Gaullist France during the General's absence from power from 1946 to 1958. They had been supporters of a French Algeria, but when Algerian independence became inevitable, a number of them rediscovered New France and turned their energies to pressing the cause of a Quebec with its own international personality. Jurgensen was one of them.

He undertook to explain to me the General's view of the future of Quebec by calling to my attention the text of the press conference where it stated that "it goes without saying that France is ready to entertain with the whole of Canada, which will take on a new form, the best relations possible." According to Jurgensen, the General foresaw the constitution of Canada developing toward an Austro-Hungarian solution; in the Austro-Hungarian empire both Austria and Hungary were sovereign but each owed allegiance to the same emperor and they had mutual defence commitments to each other. (It was never clear to me who in this scenario was to play the role of emperor in the New Canada: the Queen?) When I suggested that this solution appeared to be very similar to the sovereignty thesis of René Lévesque, Jurgensen nodded his head. It seemed ironic to me that De Gaulle was supporting a solution for the future of Quebec that had been formulated by a political opponent of his "friend" Daniel Johnson.

At the Elysée Palace one of the key posts was held by the Political Counsellor, whose task it was to act as a conduit on foreign affairs to and from De Gaulle. At a time when most matters of foreign policy were the "reserved" sphere of influence of the President, the post acquired added weight and the incumbent, René de la Saussaye Saint-Légier, was an important source for the latest thoughts of the General. He was also the contact for the Quebec Delegation.

De Gaulle had taken exception to a phrase in Ambassador Léger's presentation of Letters of Credence in 1964 and since then, the Ambassador had had limited access to the President. There had been three ministers in two years at the Embassy, so that when I arrived, there was no contact with the Elysée. Fortunately, one of my colleagues had served as a young officer in Rome with Saint-Légier and he suggested he give a small dinner party where I could meet Saint-Légier and arrange to call on him. This was done, and our subsequent meetings proved useful, even if they made for unpleasant reading in Ottawa. I always found Saint-Légier agreeable to do business with. He was straightforward, and did not try to sugar-coat the General's attitude toward the federal government. He will reappear frequently in this narrative.

Shortly after my arrival, Ambassador Léger asked me to replace him at a goodbye dinner being given by the France-Canada Association for Pierre de Menthon, the new French Consul General in Quebec City. Since many of those who were present were strong supporters of De Gaulle's views, I could not resist, when asked to say a few words, expressing the hope that during his holidays de Menthon would take the opportunity to visit the rest of Canada in order to better appreciate the nature of the country. This sally was greeted with a distinct hush, and if I had known what De Gaulle's instructions to De Menthon were I would not have bothered.

De Gaulle had told De Menthon that he was not, like his predecessors, being sent as Consul General at Quebec, but rather as Consul General to the Quebec government.[2] He wanted the French of Canada to know that France was back. The Consulate General would no longer depend on the French Embassy in Ottawa; it would be responsible for the French office in Montreal; and it would have its own direct communications with the French Foreign Ministry. Its size would be considerably increased (it in fact went from twelve to sixty employees). He went on to tell De Menthon that those who argued that there were economic dangers in independence were merely finding an excuse for doing nothing—the U.S. would continue its investments. This seemed to be in direct contradiction with De Gaulle's belief that the U.S. posed a global threat to the French language and culture. The instructions clearly demonstrate that what De Gaulle was doing was creating a second French Embassy in all but name on Canadian territory.

My opposite number at the American Embassy came to see me with his message to Washington on De Gaulle's Press Conference. Not being an expert in Franco-Canadian relations, he wanted to check out his facts. We were old colleagues, having served together in Stalin's Moscow. The Americans had asked for an explanation from the Quai of the press conference, not from Jurgensen, whom they found too fanatical, but from his deputy. Not surprisingly they had received the same line as I had from Jurgensen: that there was to be a sovereign Quebec but not an independent Quebec; once Quebec was sovereign it could negotiate future economic relations with the rest of Canada—the Austro-Hungarian model.

My friend also told me of a recent address given by the Quebec Delegate General to the Princeton Club of Paris, at which he had made the following points: the Quebec Delegation had the same privileges and immunities as other diplomatic missions in Paris, but without the designation of Embassy; the Delegate General could see anyone in French official circles, from the Head of State on down; personal relations with the Canadian Embassy were friendly but there was no official relationship between the two missions; sovereignty does not mean independence and a new constitutional relationship must come into being. His personal view was that it would be similar to the German Confederation. The American comment was that the Delegate General did not specify what stage in German history he was referring to. Finally, in talking to his hosts after his address he caused annoyance by telling them that the Quebec Delegation in Paris had the same status as the Delegation of North Vietnam.

At that period, I also saw a Belgian friend who was at the time Minister of French Language Education in the Belgian government and a great admirer of France. He said that his political friends in Wallonia (the French-speaking part of Belgium) were increasingly concerned about De Gaulle's activities in Canada and the creation of an international Francophone movement. The autonomist Parti Wallon had gained seven seats in the last election, due partly to a sudden influx of money from France. The Party, like its Flemish counterpart, was primarily made up of intellectuals who treated all questions from a nationalist and linguistic point of view, whereas in Wallonia the real problems were social and economic. His colleagues feared that the General might ask to visit Belgium, and they considered with horror the possibility of him shouting "Vive La Wallonie libre" from the city hall in Liège.

NOTES

1. Claude Morin, *L'Art de l'impossible*, 75.
2. Pierre de Menthon, *Je Témoigne*, 16-18.

3

LA FRANCOPHONIE AND THE
OUTBREAK OF HOSTILITIES:
THE GABON AFFAIR

AS QUEBEC'S RELATIONS with France progressed, so did the expectation that relations could be developed with the newly independent former colonies of France and Belgium, thus providing a wider international stage for independent Quebec action. When the French Education Minister, Alain Peyrefitte, visited Quebec in September 1967, he told Quebec ministers of the regular series of meetings between the Education Ministers of France and the former colonies to discuss continuing developments in French education and French aid in the educational field. The meetings took place once a year in an African capital, with a follow-up meeting in Paris.

There was particular interest in Quebec in these meetings, for they would provide an opportunity to keep up to date with the evolution of Francophone education in the wider international sphere. They had an additional attraction: they took place in an international forum, and since education was an exclusive provincial jurisdiction under the British North America Act, here was an opportunity to establish Quebec's international personality. If this move succeeded, Quebec could go on to claim independent standing in other educational and culture-related international organizations such as UNESCO.

Certain senior African leaders, particularly President Léopold Senghor of Senegal, had been interested for some years in the establishment of a wider international community—La Francophonie—where French-speaking or partially French-speaking countries could cooperate in a variety of cultural, youth and technical exchanges and also develop an aid agency (the Agence Francophone) that would give access to sources of aid not exclusively from France. These leaders also envisaged the evolution of La Francophonie toward a forum for regular informal political consultations, along the lines of the Commonwealth.

Quebec wished to participate in all these activities in its own right. The federal government maintained that in accordance with international law, there could only be one government representing Canada but that provinces could, in conjunction with the federal government, formulate Canadian policy for La Francophonie and participate in its various programs. These two institutions, the Education Conferences and La Francophonie, were to provide one of the main battlegrounds throughout my years in Paris: a continuing struggle between Quebec attempting, with wholehearted French assistance, to establish its international personality and Ottawa, insisting on its right to represent all of Canada.

Late in 1967 the Quebec government asked France to arrange for an invitation to the next meeting of Education Ministers to be sent directly to Quebec, without informing Ottawa. Quebec thought itself to be in a strong position, not only because of De Gaulle's Canadian policy but also because of perceived weakness in the federal government: Prime Minister Pearson was expected to announce his resignation soon, and the Liberal government would then be fully preoccupied with a leadership campaign. Quebec was also fortunate in that the next Education Ministers' Conference was to be held in Libreville, the capital of Gabon. President Bongo, the local dictator, was a great admirer of De Gaulle and was likely to do whatever the General asked.

Ottawa was aware of Quebec's intentions and realized that a long campaign lay ahead if an eventual compromise between Ottawa and Quebec was to be found. Therefore, the first move was to send a letter from Prime Minister Pearson to Premier Johnson on December 1, 1967 stating the willingness of the federal government to have Quebec representatives as members of Canadian delegations to international conferences. Ottawa also wished to establish cooperation with Quebec in the area of La Francophonie, in order to achieve a common Canadian policy and to ensure a strong Quebec participation, within Canadian delegations, to the various future conferences on La Francophonie. Quebec did not reply, for it was pursuing a different objective: namely, a separate invitation from Gabon to be the sole Canadian participant at the meeting in Libreville. Claude Morin admitted that the Pearson letter might be useful later in negotiations with Ottawa. [1]

Paul Martin raised the question of a Canadian presence at Libreville with Couve de Murville at their meeting on December 13, dealing with the General's press conference. Couve's reply was to the effect that he found meetings on La Francophonie "a waste of time" but that in any case they were outside his jurisdiction. They were indeed, as all matters relating to the former colonies, handled by the services of Jacques Foccart, the intelligence professional who worked in the Elysée Palace for De Gaulle.

The same evening in Paris Ambassador Léger, on instructions, saw De Bettencourt, the Secretary of State for Foreign Affairs responsible for Quebec affairs. The Ambassador stated once again the federal government's competence in international affairs and its interest in La Francophonie. He pointed out that Ottawa also had responsibility for about one million French-speaking Canadians living outside Quebec, and had consulted the provinces concerned (New Brunswick, Ontario and Manitoba). Canada officially asked for French support for the attendance of a group of Canadian observers, which would include representatives from these provinces, at the Gabon Conference. De Bettencourt took the easy way out by saying that it was not France that was doing the inviting but Gabon, and we should speak to them. Léger replied that we had done so but were approaching France as well because we knew that France had already been consulted on Canadian participation, and this was the basis for our request that it support the attendance of the group of observers. De Bettencourt would have known at this time that his government had already successfully persuaded President Bongo to invite Quebec. Léger also took this opportunity to warn the French that Ottawa would be taking a similar attitude to all education meetings and to any forthcoming conferences to create La Francophonie.

Meanwhile, in Quebec, the government was becoming increasingly concerned that the expected separate invitation had not arrived. Claude Morin was sufficiently worried that he ventured into enemy territory, visiting the French Ambassador in Ottawa to set out the Quebec position once again and ask what had happened to the invitation. It finally arrived on January 17, 1968 from the Gabonese Embassy in Washington and Cardinal, the Quebec Minister of Education, was quickly packed off with instructions to avoid the press before his arrival in Gabon.

At the beginning of 1968, all participants at the Education Conference were officially informed by Canadian diplomatic note of our position that under the Canadian constitution the federal government was the sole representative on international affairs. To follow this up, and maintain pressure, Ambassador Léger saw De Bettencourt again on January 5, repeating the Canadian position and making it clear that any invitation addressed to a member of the federal union that was Canada, rather than to the federal government, was a direct interference in Canadian internal affairs. De Bettencourt was clearly uncomfortable. Léger told Ottawa that unless the federal government secured an agreement with Quebec, its request for an observer group would be refused, and that a Quebec presence at Libreville was likely.

At this same meeting, De Bettencourt told Léger that the Africans wanted the first conference to create La Francophonie soon after the meeting in Gabon, but because of the preparations involved the French had put this off until the autumn. He also said that since this meeting was of a broader scope, invitations could go to the Ministers of Education of New Brunswick, Ontario and Manitoba as well as to the Quebec Minister. Léger confined himself to remarking that this new conference was clearly intergovernmental, and therefore only the federal government could be invited and should decide the nature of the Canadian delegation.

The federal government now had a clear warning of the much greater confrontation that lay ahead. As Léger told Ottawa, the French had now revealed their game, which was to bypass Ottawa on matters of education and possibly culture as well, and to deal directly with the provinces. Our problem was that La Francophonie could not be created without France and De Gaulle considered that Ottawa was not a valid interlocutor. What had happened was that the Canadian constitutional dispute had now been exported to Africa, and Canada would have to try to obtain African support for its case while continuing the dialogue with Quebec and France.

This first phase of the Gabon affair closed on January 15 in Paris. During a lunch in honor of a visiting Canadian Cabinet Minister, Jean-Luc Pepin, who was to open an exhibition of Modern Canadian Art, De Bettencourt informed us that the French government had advised the Gabon government to invite Quebec to the Education Ministers' Conference.

In Gabon we had no resident Ambassador, and the new Ambassador had not yet presented his credentials, so the Gabonese had an easy time of it. They first pretended they had made a mistake in not sending the invitation to Ottawa. Our Ambassador said in that case he was authorized by Ottawa to ask for an official invitation and to accept it immediately. This forced the Gabonese to fall back on the excuse that since the new Canadian Ambassador had not presented his credentials, he could not officially come to Gabon.

The Conference took place with Quebec flags flying and congratulations from the French delegation to the Gabonese for having treated Quebec as a full participant. Cardinal, the head of the Quebec delegation, received the "Order of the Green Elephant," and Ottawa suspended diplomatic relations with Gabon. Ottawa had lost the first round and had to expect a sequel in a few months time, when the follow-up conference would be held in Paris. There was something piquant about General De Gaulle's exploitation of Gabon. After giving it its independence, he then pressured its President personally to follow his wishes on the grounds that, as a former French colony, it should help another former French colony to become independent.

FOREIGN AID TO FRENCH-SPEAKING AFRICA

If Canada was to establish itself in French-speaking Africa as a legitimate player, it would have to do more than make diplomatic protests to France and the Africans. Pending an agreement between Ottawa and Quebec on how Canada was to be represented in international francophone institutions, there was one area in which Ottawa could act quickly—foreign aid.

With the break-up of the British, French and Belgian empires in Africa (the only continent where there was a linguistic division similar to that in Canada), a large number of small, newly independent states came into being and sought foreign assistance. Canada had provided some assistance to the Commonwealth countries of Africa. Now consideration had to be given the countries of the former French and Belgian empires, which were also members of those same international francophone institutions where French and Quebec action posed a threat to Ottawa's ability to act as sole spokesperson for Canada in international affairs.

After the acquisition of independence by the French African nations, some Canadian aid had been provided by both Canada and Quebec, but clearly a much larger program, with proper financing, was required. To achieve this goal meant there would have to be cooperation between Ottawa and Quebec. The former had the finances and some personnel, the latter the bulk of the necessary human resources, particularly in education. After long negotiations a *modus vivendi* was reached, and the Canadian International Development Agency acquired a new French-speaking capability, while Quebec continued to provide smaller amounts of aid on its own. Thus, Canada started to project to the Third World a truer image of itself than it had done previously, as a country able to provide aid in the languages of its two founding peoples.

There was clear evidence that the African countries concerned would welcome a source of aid other than from France, particularly one that had access to North American expertise and technology. The first step had to be a comprehensive examination of the needs of these countries in terms of available Canadian resources and personnel. It was decided to send an investigatory mission led by a senior political figure; this was Lionel Chevrier, a former minister in the Pearson Cabinet. Because of France's overwhelming position in its former colonies, any Canadian aid program should ideally be carried out in consultation with France. Given our relations and the possibility that France did not want interference from outside, French cooperation seemed unlikely. The only way to find out was to enquire, so the French government was asked if it would receive the Chevrier Mission for consultations before the team set out for Africa.

To our surprise the French agreed to see the Mission—in the middle of February 1968—and to our even greater surprise all the doors were opened, so that Chevrier and his team met with the French ministers and senior officials involved in the various French aid programs. We were told that Couve De Murville had given his approval, but knowing his loyalty to the General and his lack of interest in La Francophonie, we assumed that he must have received authorization from the Elysée. It was clear from our meetings with the French that those concerned with aid programs were willing to share the burden and consult on a regular basis, but they would not have been so open without approval from the highest political level. One possible explanation is that Quebec, since it was cooperating in this area with Ottawa, considered it in its own interest that the Chevrier Mission be received, and so informed the French. In any case, De Gaulle's thoughts on this incident remain a mystery. Chevrier was of course delighted, and spoke to the press of a new era of cooperation between France and Canada. Our reaction at the Embassy was more sober. While the visit had gone well, and it was right that the Mission had come to Paris, the fact remained that our fundamental differences with France over Quebec's international personality remained. Indeed, the next crisis was only weeks away.

MEETING OF THE MINISTERS OF EDUCATION IN PARIS

The Education Ministers' meeting followed automatically from the Gabon Conference, so the French took the line that no new invitations were necessary. Quebec should attend automatically because it had participated in the previous conference. We also knew from our own sources that the General had said he had no objections if Quebec wished to attend, and that nothing should be done to displease Quebec. Ottawa was once again the loser, but it was still necessary to go through the diplomatic ritual if Canada was to maintain its juridical position and be ready to fight another day. All this took place in the middle of the Liberal convention to choose a new prime minister.

On March 29, 1968 the French Ambassador in Ottawa was called in by Marcel Cadieux and told that the forthcoming meeting raised serious problems for Canada, and that if participation were limited to Quebec, in disregard of the rights of the federal government and the partially French-speaking provinces, there would be serious repercussions. By this time Premier Robichaud of New Brunswick, in consultation with Ottawa, had written to the French and Quebec governments expressing interest in the education conferences. On the same day in Paris, the Political Director of the Foreign Ministry had confirmed to the Embassy the French line, that the Paris Meeting was a mere extension of the Conference in Gabon and that since Quebec had attended in Gabon, it was natural that it should attend in Paris. Ambassador Léger replied that such facile "solutions" solved nothing, and that if Quebec participated, then from Ottawa's stand-point, France was once again interfering in Canadian domestic affairs.

In Canada Prime Minister Pearson had written three times to Premier Johnson, most recently on April 5, the day before the Leadership Convention, attempting to open a dialogue and offering the Chairmanship of the Canadian delegation to the Quebec Minister of Education. An answer finally came after the leadership convention; in Quebec, presumably, they thought it smarter tactically to reply to a lame-duck prime minister. Though full of compliments about Pearson's role in constitutional talks, Premier Johnson refused the proposal made by Ottawa, and said that Quebec intended to attend the Paris Meeting separately.

On April 8 Pierre Trudeau became Canada's new prime minister and called an election. I had known him socially in Ottawa when I was a young Foreign Service Officer and he was in the Privy Council. I had been in Moscow in 1952 when he turned up there, and we had lunched together when I was in London, disagreeing amiably about the merits of Fidel Castro. In a personal note that I wrote at the time of his selection as Liberal leader, I expressed the belief that, if he won the election, the nature and tone of our disputes with France could worsen. It was true he had studied in France and had an affection for the country, but his contempt for Quebec's nationalist ideologues, his federalist option, his dislike of losing an argument, particularly with a "mother country," and his student-like tendency to give a "smart reply" would, to say the least, not be pleasing to the General. It would be a new experience for the French government to have an adversary who could give as good as he got, and in their own language. There was a balancing factor in the new Trudeau government in the appointment of Mitchell Sharp to External Affairs. His experience, quiet firmness and negotiating strengths were to be invaluable.

Three days after the convention, we were instructed to present a note to the French requesting that Canada be invited to attend the Education Conference. Our note reiterated the position, under the Canadian constitution, that only the federal government could be invited to conferences of an international or intergovernmental nature. It informed the French that the Canadian delegation would be presided over by the Quebec Minister of Education, and would have amongst its participants representatives from other interested provinces, such as New Brunswick. The government also advised the Embassy that Ottawa did not at this time intend to escalate the dispute nor publicly react to it. The new Prime Minister wished to have immediate consultations with Ambassador Léger on the whole gamut of our relations with France. He was to leave Paris discreetly, so that his departure could not be interpreted as a diplomatic gesture by Ottawa. I would explain to the French a few days later that his return to Canada was a routine visit for leave and consultations.

On Good Friday (April 19, 1968) I was called in by De Bettencourt to receive the French oral reply to our note.[1] Once again I was treated to the French thesis that since this was an extension of the Gabon Conference, which Quebec had attended, it was natural that Quebec should attend the Paris Meeting. I was left with the impression that the French considered Gabon to be a precedent and that there would be no further invitations, merely reminders to those who had participated in previous meetings. If this was their position, it left the partially French-speaking Canadian provinces, as well as Ottawa, out on a limb.

De Bettencourt concluded by noting the reported remarks of the new Canadian Prime Minister about a possible meeting with De Gaulle: "He did not know what Trudeau had in mind, but the French preferred to take no action at this time to add fuel to the fire." My conclusions were that France would continue to abide by Quebec's wishes unless there was an agreement between Ottawa and the province, and that since a new prime minister had been installed and an early Canadian election was in

tion, while De Gaulle's power was to be greatly weakened by the events of May 1968.

NOTES

1. Paris Embassy Telegram to Ottawa, no. 1321, April 19, 1968.
2. Cabinet Minutes, nos. 42-68, 43-68, April 28 and May 2, 1968.
3. Paris Embassy Telegram to Ottawa, no. 1504, May 14, 1968.

4

THE TRIALS OF AN ELDER STATESMAN
THE EVENTS OF MAY 1968

FROM THE CANADIAN STANDPOINT the Events of May, which shook France for several weeks, were important as an indicator that De Gaulle's political position was by no means secure. What began as yet another student protest against the "system" (similar to those in America and Western Europe during the sixties), escalated into an occupation of the Sorbonne and of barricades in the student quarter of Paris, thanks to some degree of popular support and to the government's unsure reaction. Seeing the inability of authorities to counter the students, the unions, particularly the powerful Communist-led Confédération Général du Travail, called a general strike and started demonstrations in the working-class sections of Paris, and in other parts of the country.

The General came through the crisis and rescued the political system he had created, but French confidence in his policies at home and abroad had been shaken. His own view of the world, even before May 1968, had been deeply pessimistic. In late March, I had paid one of my regular visits to Saint-Légier at the Elysée, where I was treated to a detailed account of De Gaulle's views. As he saw it, every 20 or 30 years since the French Revolution there had been a period of general uncertainty, when a series of developments converged, creating an unwillingness to accept the conventional truths of the day and a desire to change the accepted order.

He believed that we were now entering such a period, during which the war in Vietnam could escalate and lead to the use of nuclear weapons. As a major world power, the U.S. was, because of its Vietnam involvement and its internal racial problems, increasingly uncertain of its role and unwilling to accept the fact that many of its allies no longer saw the world through American eyes. In the economic sphere of the international structure, he was afraid that restrictive measures taken by nations acting individually or in groups could cause the collapse of the present monetary and commercial system.

The lesson De Gaulle derived from all this was that Europe must evolve on its own, so as to be as independent as possible from the U.S. The Franco-West German alliance was therefore essential. Insofar as Eastern Europe was concerned, De Gaulle foresaw no traumatic or immediate change. No matter what liberal developments might take place in Poland or Czechoslovakia, the Russians, if they came to believe that their own security was affected, would intervene—as in fact they did, five months later in Czechoslovakia.

At the time, I was inclined to find these views fairly typical of an aging politician approaching the end of his term, inclined to see catastrophe because he would no longer be there. De Gaulle's assessment of Eastern Europe and his continuing belief in the Franco-German alliance confirmed our impression at the Embassy that he had no intention of leaving the North Atlantic Alliance, at least for a while.

In retrospect, what is fascinating about his predictions was his reference to "an unwillingness to accept the conventional truths of the day and a desire to change the accepted order." He clearly did not expect that such a series of developments in France were only a few weeks away and that they would shake his regime to its very core.

Foreigners in Paris could only be spectators throughout this extraordinary period when a modern industrial society slowly brought itself to a halt. We could visit the Sorbonne or the Odeon Theatre and listen to the students and intellectuals in tempestuous debate and wonder if we were seeing the start of a new French Revolution. It struck me that what we were really seeing was a psychodrama. Raymond Aron, the French political thinker, described it best as "revolutionary verbalism." Most nights there were demonstrations and barricades in the Latin Quarter and from our windows we could hear the 'Poum Poum' of tear gas grenades as the gendarmerie and paramilitary CRS tried to restore order.[1]

Paris was isolated from the rest of the country. Food was allowed in at night by arrangement between the farmers and the unions; electricity was periodically cut off, except during meal hours; and the main sources of information were state radio and television which, freed from government controls, were providing uncensored news and comment.

At the Embassy, our prime concern was with the many stranded Canadians and busloads of tourists, and with ways of getting them out of France. As the situation worsened we had to plan for the possibility of some form of civil war. Embassy cars stood ready to be commandeered, and large supplies of gasoline were stored in the Embassy compound in case it became necessary to evacuate dependants and non-essential staff to Belgium.

Many weeks before, my wife and I had arranged a dinner party that would include a senior member of the Foreign Ministry, De Gaulle's press spokesperson and Saint-Légier. We decided to go ahead and see who would turn up, and whether we could learn what was going on. It was a dramatic evening. The Foreign Ministry man phoned to say, very stuffily, that under the circumstances it would not be appropriate to dine out. The press spokesperson, as a result of a large Communist union demonstration the previous day, was in a state of panic. He was sure that the Communists were about to take over, and that as a member of the Elysée staff he was in physical danger. He came to dinner but spent the evening canvassing views on the best way to remove his money, his family and himself from France. Probably aware that he had not distinguished himself that evening he never spoke to me again.

Saint-Légier was very late, but he came, announcing dramatically as he entered the room: "We have lost him." This was the day when the General disappeared from Paris without informing anyone (except probably Pompidou) where he was going or what he intended to do. According to Saint-Légier, when the General returned from Romania he thought the students' movement, because it represented a small minority in society, could be dealt with by administrative means and the promise of a referendum. His reaction to the strike of the unions was that it was a classic attempt to use a providential situation to obtain greater benefits. Despite the advice of his ministers and personal staff, he had refused to accept that the regime was in crisis until a few days previously. What would he do next? Our conversation that night lasted into the small hours.

We learned next day that the General had once again used suprise tactics. He had flown to the headquarters of the French army of the Rhine to ensure that he had military support if he needed to use it. He had spent the night at his home in the country and then returned to Paris, and appeared in uniform on television to announce the dissolution of Parliament, a round of new elections, and to call for support from those who believed in civic action. This was followed shortly by a mammoth Gaullist demonstration in the centre of Paris in support of the regime. Then came the Whitsun long weekend, when large amounts of gasoline were made available. Breathing a sigh of relief, Parisians jumped in their cars and took to the countryside. The crisis was over.

The Events of May had shown that the Gaullist government had feet of clay. More importantly, it showed a De Gaulle unsure of himself, overtaken by events and having to rely on his prime minister to run a country partly in revolt while he tried to make up his mind. What effect would these events have on France's relations with Canada? Since one of the main reasons for the students' revolt was the inefficacy of the French educational system, the Canadian provinces concerned would be taking a much harder look at French assistance. On the other hand, the General was still in power and would not change his policy toward Canada or Quebec.

That De Gaulle had been slow to accept the fact that his regime was in danger was demonstrated by his agreement, in the middle of the May Events, that the often-postponed visit of Premier Johnson would take place in July. Ambassador Léger was instructed by Prime Minister Trudeau to ensure a Canadian presence at the main ceremonies and was asked to invite the Premier to a reception at the Embassy, as he had done on the previous visit in 1966. In June, Johnson announced his visit to France for the early part of July, and we learned that he would be at the General's side for the July 14 Parade. With Ottawa's accord, Léger decided to leave town for this occasion and have me represent Canada. This would avoid an incident, which the press would play up, in which the President of France would honor a Canadian provincial Premier accompanied by his Delegate General, while the Ambassador of Canada would be left with the rest of the diplomatic corps. The Ambassador's absence would be seen as a quiet protest by Canada to the latest challenge from the General.

Fortunately, none of this was to take place. I called on Saint-Légier to review where our relations stood in the light of recent events, and while waiting, noticed Chapdelaine and André Patry, a civil servant from Quebec, leaving Saint-Légier's office with rather long faces. Saint-Légier told me that in the light of the May Events, De Gaulle would be concentrating on domestic reforms, and while there would be no change in foreign policy there would be no new initiatives. This observation applied to Canada, where there was a new prime minister, and he understood Premier Johnson was seriously ill (which explained the presence of his previous visitors). It looked therefore as if the General would leave us alone for a while: for two months to be exact.

Saint-Légier also told me that the General firmly believed that the recent crisis had been caused by the dependence of the French government on the conservative establishment and the business community, by which I took him to mean Pompidou and his friends. Fundamental changes were required in the management of the universities, factories and ministries. Saint-Légier pointed out that throughout the crisis there had been no questioning of De Gaulle's foreign policy, but he then admitted that it was by no means clear that France could maintain that foreign policy, because of the demonstrated fragility of French society: "We are not in as strong a position as we or others thought we were."[2]

The new government, announced a week later, showed clearly that the reforms were to be De Gaulle's alone. Pompidou was replaced as prime minister by the faithful but unimaginative Couve De Murville; Debré, equally faithful, was given Foreign Affairs, and apart from a few relatively unknown Gaullists with social concerns the rest were a mix of the usual "barons." One minor nomination was to cause Canada considerable problems over the next two years. The new Secretary of State for Foreign Affairs, who would therefore be the minister responsible for Quebec, was Jean De Lipkowski, an ambitious former foreign service officer known to some of my colleagues who had served with him in China. His propensity to talk before thinking, which will become evident later in this book, had earned him the nickname of "Lippy the Lip."

NOTES

1. The May Events were extraordinary but by no means unusual in French history. In writing about the Revolution of 1830 Chateaubriand, in his *Mémoires d'outre tombe*, wrote "Barricades are the fortified strong points that are part of the Parisian genius, one finds them during all our troubles since Charles V [1500-1558] to the present day." [Au reste les barricades sont des retranchements qui appartiennent au génie parisien; on les retrouve dans tous nos troubles depuis Charles V. jusqu'à nos jours.]
2. Embassy Paris Telegrams to Ottawa, nos. 2636, 2637, July 5, 1968.

5

A TRANSATLANTIC SLANGING MATCH
THE ROSSILLON AFFAIR

THE GENERAL INAUGURATED the next brouhaha between France and Canada at a press conference on September 8, 1968. In answer to a question from the ever eager correspondent of *La Presse* as to whether, in view of the Events of May and the fact that there was a new Canadian Prime Minister, there would be a change in France's attitude to Quebec, De Gaulle replied "Certainly not." This was hardly surprising, but more gratuitous was his statement regarding the Nigerian civil war in Biafra: "One sometimes replaces colonization by a certain concept of federation—one sees it in Canada, Cyprus, Rhodesia and Malaysia."

Prime Minister Trudeau reacted in kind the next day in the House of Commons and at greater length at a press conference on September 11. A few excerpts will give the flavour: "It may be easy to criticize such federations as Nigeria but it seems to me that the U.S. has not been weakened by its form of government.... I have read that even the General, who has not succumbed to federalism, is thinking of reforms that involve decentralization. Does this mean that the French Government wishes to give a little more autonomy to the Bretons, the Basques and the Alsatians who want a greater respect for their cultural rights and to be less colonized by Paris?.... I have the impression that the French Government has been shaken by the Events of last May and has not quite recovered itself, and therefore French logic is lacking at the government level."

All this was bad enough, but a much more serious affair had developed in Manitoba involving Philippe Rossillon, the Chairman of the High Commision for the Defence and Expansion of the French Language, attached to the Office of the French Prime Minister. At the press conference Trudeau had seemed intent on dealing with this man's activities in a way that would both embarrass the French government and ensure that there would be no repetition of such behaviour.

Rossillon was well known for his previous activities in Canada and had been the subject of complaint to the French in the past. He was an affluent young man, an early member of *Patrie et Progrès*, who used his Commission (of which he seemed to be the only active member) as cover for his personal approach to helping French-speaking Canadians. He had close ties with senior Quebec civil servants and for a while with some members of the terrorist Front de Libération du Québec.

His latest escapades in Canada had commenced during the visit of Alain Peyrefitte, the former French Minister of Education, to Quebec in September 1967. At that time, Rossillon had slipped away to Moncton without informing his own Embassy, much less the federal or provincial governments. In Moncton he met with a small group of Acadians from the Société L'Assomption. These Acadians wanted help in the general area of education—some worked at the University of Moncton—as well as subsidies for the newspaper *L'Evangéline* which was in financial difficulties. Rossillon does not seem to have realized—or perhaps it did not concern him—that this group in Moncton were not representative of Acadians in general nor on particularly good terms with the Premier of New Brunswick, Louis Robichaud, the first Acadian to hold this office. He encouraged them to ask for French assistance and helped them write a letter to General De Gaulle which he then undertook to deliver. An invitation to visit Paris was forthcoming and the four Acadians appeared in Paris in January 1968.

The group was seen by a variety of officials and ministers and received at lunch by De Gaulle, who promised assistance. Overwhelmed by their reception and the press coverage, they then came to the Embassy to tell us what had occurred. Meanwhile, the reaction to the visit in New Brunswick was highly negative, as could have been predicted. There was a backlash from that part of the the English-speaking population who had never acknowledged that Acadians had a language and culture of their own, while many Acadians were concerned that the considerable progress they had made in the province (exemplified by an Acadian Premier and progress toward bilingual status) could be jeopardized. Rossillon, however, had accomplished one thing; he had obtained De Gaulle's approval for helping a French Canadian group outside Quebec. This was progress of a sort, but the General would not admit that such help was already envisaged in the Franco-Canadian Cultural Agreement of 1965 (see page 6). He still considered that Ottawa had no role in any assistance that France might provide to French-speaking Canadians.

The next stage in this sequence of events was an order from De Gaulle to the Quai d'Orsay to visit New Brunswick to see what help could be provided. Jean Basdevant, Director General of Cultural Relations, and Jurgensen as Director of the North American Department, led a large delegation that descended on the province at the end of March 1968, travelling via Quebec and bypassing Ottawa. Since this was a delegation with high visibility its members could not proceed to Moncton and make arrangements with their friends there while ignoring the government of New Brunswick. When Premier Robichaud learned of the visit he issued an official invitation, requesting the French delegation to come first to Fredericton, consulted with Ottawa, and asked that a federal official be in attendance. The Premier had three objectives: to accept French assistance, provided it was furnished through the channels envisaged by the Cultural Agreement between Canada and France; to make clear to the French that there could not be arrangements between Paris and a private group in New Brunswick—such arrangements had to involve the provincial government in the first instance; and that New Brunswick wished, as a partially Francophone province, to be invited to the meetings of the Francophone Ministers of Education. [1]

The French Delegation was not pleased with this approach but when they objected, the Premier treated them to a lecture on relations between the two linguistic groups in the province and the need to ensure the continuation of a harmonious relationship between them while Acadians made progress with their own French-speaking institutions. Premier Robichaud had, in effect, taken the visit out of the hands of the group in Moncton and clearly established that cultural and linguistic relations with France would in future be dealt with through proper channels. He also implied (despite French protestations) that at this stage in their history Acadians would not appreciate any intellectual imperialism from the other side of the Atlantic. The Premier failed to achieve the last of his three objectives. He handed Basdevant a letter for the French Foreign Minister—he had consulted Pearson about this—requesting an invitation to the Education Conferences. Basdevant took it without comment, but in fact New Brunswick was not invited. Quebec wanted no rival provinces while it was trying to establish its international presence.

Rossillon, quite pleased with his success in Moncton and ignoring the Basdevant experience, decided that his next sortie should be in Manitoba. At the end of August 1968 he turned up in the small village of St. Pierre, outside Winnipeg, some of whose inhabitants he had met when they were visiting Paris. He then convened a wide range of French-speaking Manitobans to hear their views on how France could help them, and as he had done in Moncton, he encouraged them to write General De Gaulle soliciting an invitation to Paris. That so many attended Rossillon's meeting is hardly surprising, considering how the French Canadians of Manitoba had been treated during the previous hundred years.

Rossillon had proceeded without informing his own Embassy, much less Ottawa or the Manitoba government. His hosts, however, informed the Secretary of State's Department in Ottawa and asked that a federal official take part in the conversations. René Préfontaine, from that Department, went immediately to Winnipeg and informed the Manitoban authorities of his presence. Derek Bedson, the Secretary of the Manitoba Cabinet, called in Rossillon, who appeared reluctantly, claiming that he was on a private visit. He was told that Manitoba, while welcoming French assistance, would prefer that such activities be carried out under the Franco-Canadian Cultural Agreement.[2] At this point Rossillon slipped away to Quebec, but he had overplayed his hand and by the time the storm was over he could no longer engage independently in Canadian forays.

At the press conference of September 11, Trudeau had made the following statement:

Nothing could be more harmful to the acceptance of the bilingual character of Canada in the provinces where French-speaking Canadians are in a minority than having the agents of a foreign state coming into the country and agitating as it were to get the citizens of that particular province to act in a given way ... there is a cultural agreement with France which covers precisely the type of activity which Rossillon is interested in ... the French government officially can talk to the Canadian government to promote certain cultural activities of the French-speaking people in Canada, and it is rather distasteful that the French government should not act directly through the agreement but should do so in this underhanded and surreptitious way.[3]

The press combined the word "agent" (which Rossillon was, since he was attached to the Office of the French Prime Minister), and the word "surreptitious" (which did describe his activities, since he had informed no one of his activities in Canada), and turned him into "a secret agent," a spy, which he was not. The Canadian Press agency also produced a list of some of Rossillon's more dubious contacts in Quebec, which they could only have obtained from the Canadian security authorities. All this made it easier for the French to say that the Canadian Prime Minister was badly informed and that his reaction was out of proportion. It also made it possible for the French Foreign Minister to state that a visit between Prime Minister Trudeau and General De Gaulle was unlikely under the circumstances. It had always been unlikely, but the French now had an excuse to say so.

Prime Minister Trudeau appears to have decided that things had gone too far, for he made a statement in the House of Commons a few days later, on September 16, designed to put Franco-Canadian relations in their proper perspective: "We want close relations with France, particularly at a time when the Federal Government is engaged in strengthening the roots of Canadians of the French language throughout the country. We welcome any help France or other countries might wish to give in this task, providing such help is not given in such a way as to sow differences between Canadians—because this question is of fundamental importance the Canadian Government considers that it must be informed and consulted by the French Government on such activities as those that have recently made the headlines."[4]

In Paris the next day, a gentleman called "Broussine," who published a regular subsidized tract that said things that the French government could not say in public, wrote a violent attack against Trudeau. Trudeau was accused of conducting an anti-French campaign, not only because he disagreed with De Gaulle's policies toward Canada, but also with De Gaulle's remarks about federal states: "Why is Trudeau carrying on such a campaign? No doubt to stop relations between France and Quebec; if he continues in this way he risks the break-up of Canada; in fact his behaviour has probably made it impossible to establish a federation accepted by French Canadians and this will lead inevitably to the break-up of the country and the birth of a French Nation in North America."[5] These sentiments quite accurately represented the hopes of some in the Quebec Delegation and of the group of activists within the French government and bureaucracy who supported an international personality for Quebec.

My expectations concerning the Prime Minister's style and his willingness to take on the French whenever necessary had certainly been met. The Embassy's impression was that his statements had embarrassed the Quai D'Orsay to the point that they would if they could stop the transatlantic polemic. Ambassador Léger was called in by Secretary General Alphand who had been given the task, clearly distasteful to him, of defending Rossillon's "private" trip to Canada. After he had finished his brief he suggested that the matter be closed. Léger took the occasion to remind Alphand that the latest events were yet another example of the problems posed by visits of French ministers and civil servants to Canada, including Quebec, without informing Ottawa. What had happened was therefore hardly surprising, and could have been avoided by proper use of the Cultural Agreement between France and Canada.[6]

Back in Ottawa, there was also a desire to close the Rossillon affair.[7] However, it was believed, that in France the desire to close the incident represented the wishes of the Foreign Ministry and that we could not expect any changes in the attitude of De Gaulle. Shortly after these events Jean-Pierre Goyer, Parliamentary Assistant to Mitchell Sharp, came through Paris. The Embassy used the opportunity to have him make a courtesy call on De Lipkowski, the Secretary of State for Foreign Affairs. We briefed him on recent events and suggested that he tell his French opposite number that, in view of what had happened, this would be a good time for a meeting of the Franco-Canadian Cultural Commission to discuss programs of assistance to the francophone minorities outside Quebec. To our surprise De Lipkowski agreed. Our suggestion offered a way out of an embarrassing situation and had the advantage, insofar as the Quai was concerned, of ensuring that relations with Canada were controlled from the Foreign Ministry (except if the General intervened) and would not be left at the mercy of such enterprising lone rangers as Philippe Rossillon.

Oddly enough, Rossillon's activities turned out to have a positive result. The means he used were unacceptable, and the man himself untrustworthy, but the furore he created brought about a realization in Paris that, if French-speaking Canadians outside Quebec were to receive help, Rossillon's private ventures were not the appropriate means. The only proper instrument was the Cultural Agreement, which ensured representation of the provinces concerned. Of course, the French could have used this from the start, but De Gaulle had stated that Ottawa was not a proper interlocutor with regard to French-speaking Canadians. It took Rossillon's misadventures to finally convince the French government to implement, through the proper channels, the agreement on cultural exchanges that they had signed with Canada in 1965.

NOTES

1. Memorandum for File, Basdevant Mission to New Brunswick, April 11, 1968, by J. Gignac, Director of Cultural Affairs, Department of External Affairs.
2. Background Brief for Undersecretary of State for External Affairs, September 13, 1968.
3. External Affairs Telegram to Embassy Paris, W 181, September 11, 1968.
4. House of Commons, *Debates*, 6667, September 16, 1968.
5. Embassy Paris Telegram to Ottawa, no. 3477, September 17, 1968.
6. Embassy Paris Telegram to Ottawa, no. 3479, September 17, 1968.
7. Memorandum from Secretary of State for External Affairs to the Prime Minister, September 23, 1968.

6

A PREMIER DIES,
TWO PRIME MINISTERS MEET

THE FALLOUT from the Rossillon affair had just subsided when we learned that Premier Johnson had finally succumbed to his heart condition on September 26. General De Gaulle had lost his foremost Quebec interlocutor. He decided to send his new Prime Minister to the funeral, though we heard rumours he had thought seriously of going himself. He must have realized that such a trip, undertaken when he was engaged in trying to reform France, would not be understood at home, and that his reappearance in Canada could place him in unacceptable situations, such as having to meet with Prime Minister Trudeau. It was ironic that Premier Johnson's death should provide the opportunity for the first meeting between the new Prime Ministers of France and Canada: Couve De Murville, who found La Francophonie "a waste of time," and Trudeau, who strongly opposed nationalist ideologies such as contemporary Gaullism.

The two men met alone on October 4, in the apartments of the Governor General in the Quebec Citadel. The account we have of the meeting is based on a debriefing given by Trudeau to the Undersecretary of State for External Affairs, Marcel Cadieux. There were extensive discussions on international affairs of the moment, but when it came to our bilateral relations Trudeau, instead of raising the many specific problems arising between Canada and France, characteristically posed questions about the logic of French policy toward Canada. He took it for granted that France wished to support the French Fact in Canada. He was favourably disposed toward such a policy and for that reason he did not understand the logic of certain French policies. Couve replied that France wanted to assist all French-speaking Canadians and that objective should not upset the federal government.

Trudeau had no objection to such a course, and would in fact prefer to see France do more. What he found incomprehensible was the nature

At Premier Johnson's funeral, September 1968. Prime Minister Trudeau is accompanied by Jean Jacques Bertrand, acting premier of Quebec, followed by Lucien Tremblay, chief judge of Quebec, and Prime Minister Couve de Murville of France.

of specific French actions which seemed designed to weaken the presence of French-speaking Canadians in Ottawa and in the other provinces (he was referring to the Rossillon and Gabon affairs). Couve replied that Quebec was the *foyer* of French Canada, it had jurisdiction in educational matters and therefore it was logical that Quebec should participate in the international aspects of education. Trudeau pointed out that other provinces, particularly those with French-speaking minorities, had similar jurisdiction. Therefore, logically, they should not be prevented from participating in similar international meetings.

Couve avoided giving a reply by saying that France must not try to decide Canadian constitutional questions and it was not in her interest to become mixed up in disagreements between Ottawa and Quebec. Trudeau retorted that if that were indeed the case, France was interfering without wishing to; its actions had supported an increase in Quebec's international role and diminished the role and status of French-speaking Canadians in Ottawa. Couve observed that since Quebec was the *foyer* of French Canada it required an international role which was not necessary for the other provinces.

Trudeau then asked the question: "Did Couve believe that Quebec spoke for all the French-speaking Canadians outside the Province?" "No," said Couve, "but Quebec still had a particular status." "In that case" said

Trudeau, "France, by supporting Quebec's international role, was taking a position on Canadian federalism and therefore on the Canadian constitution, and, pushed to the limit this policy led to supporting separatism." Couve expressed horror at such an idea. France was against separatism, and had no interest in seeing Canada split up, for the French Fact in North America could only survive in a larger political context. If Quebec was to separate it would be assimilated, as were the Franco-Americans of New England. Trudeau terminated the exchange by saying that if this indeed was the view of the French government then he did not understand the logic of France's present policy of helping Quebec to achieve a separate international personality.

The Canadian Prime Minister's general impression of the talks was that France did not want a diplomatic break with Canada and that, if bilingualism succeeded, France would be less provocative in its support for Quebec. However, if bilingualism should fail, France would profit by having been the first to support the national and international aspirations of Quebec.[1] At the Embassy we learned from colleagues in the French Foreign Ministry that Couve made two specific comments to the French Council of Ministers on his Quebec trip. First, that the new Quebec Premier, Bertrand, was the head of a weak government and he had a number of rivals such as Cardinal and Marcel Masse. Secondly, that Quebecers were North Americans in their lifestyle despite an attachment to their French language and culture. If indeed he said this it would have been contrary to the General's favorite myth that Quebecers were the French of North America. The General, as a European nationalist, could not understand that people who were originally French could, over a period of over three hundred years, have acquired many of the standards, customs and methods of conducting business that were typical of the continent where they lived, while maintaining their separate identities through the French language and culture with little or no help from the former mother country.

At this point it is appropriate to ask where we stood a year after De Gaulle's cry of "Vive le Quebec libre!" Clearly, there had been a change in what the Marxists liked to call the "correlation of forces." Canada was no longer run by a minority government but by a majority, led by a strong federalist bilingual Prime Minister; De Gaulle had been greatly weakened by the May Events and was now, toward the end of his mandate, trying to bring in fundamental reforms; and the Union Nationale government in Quebec, which had been accustomed to a strong "Chef," was now preoccupied with leadership problems and a possible split between the old-style nationalist and the separatist wings of the party.

We have it from De Menthon, the French Consul General in Quebec, who visited De Gaulle in the autumn of 1968, that he found the General tired and disillusioned after the Events of May. Moreover he no longer believed in the general evolution toward Quebec independence that he had done so much to promote. He was nevertheless still sure that independence would come about some day.[2]

At the Embassy we wanted to know what the official attitude was at the Elysée after the Rossillon affair, Premier Johnson's death and the Couve-Trudeau meeting. I called on Saint-Légier to find out. He thought little had changed, it was a time of wait and see, with domestic preoccupations uppermost in France and new governments installing themselves in Ottawa and Quebec. The meeting between the two Prime Ministers had been "satisfactory" and therefore relations would continue as at present. When I suggested that we could continue to expect difficulties concerning Quebec's international personality, Saint-Légier agreed, since Quebec had certain ideas and France was bound to support them.[3] This confirmed our view that as long as De Gaulle was on the scene he would continue to support Quebec at the expense of Canada. France had always said that, if Ottawa and Quebec agreed on how to deal with Quebec's international personality, she would naturally accept such an agreement. This could well occur with the new premier in Quebec, but we at the Embassy remained sceptical about French acceptance; certainly the separatist supporters in Quebec and Paris would do their utmost to upset such an agreement.

An effort was now initiated to establish an area of positive cooperation in Canada's relations with France. An Aide-Mémoire on Scientific Cooperation with France, including Space Research, was prepared in Ottawa. The intention was to build on the recent sale of plutonium to France and to pre-empt French cooperation with Quebec in satellite communications, an area of mixed jurisdiction. This document was given to Foreign Minister Debré by Mitchell Sharp at their regular meeting at the United Nations on October 4, 1968. At the time Debré simply remarked that space communications had already been discussed between Premier Johnson and General De Gaulle. Sharp's action would prove useful in the light of the Cardinal visit to Paris early in 1969 (see Chapter 9).

NOTES

1. Document obtained under Access to Information Act., Ref. 1025-9-92170.
2. De Menthon, *Je Témoigne*, 18-19.
3. Embassy Paris Telegram to Ottawa, no. 3803, October 9, 1968.

7

"BUSINESS AS USUAL"

THROUGHOUT THESE RECURRENT CRISES the Canadian government, when examining its policy options toward France, would inevitably come back to the conclusion that the problem lay in Canada, between the federal government and Quebec. Until a solution or at least a *modus vivendi* was found with Quebec and until De Gaulle left the scene, Ottawa was obliged to pursue the following three objectives: protecting Canada's international sovereignty; refusing Quebec an international personality of its own; and carrying on business as usual with France. The present chapter breaks the thread of the narrative in order to give the reader an idea of what "business as usual" meant in these unusual circumstances.

The routine work of the Embassy had to continue. In spite of their disturbed relations the two countries had plenty of business to transact and the Embassy was responsible for the administration of a number of local programs. Underlying its activity there was a basic assumption: the federal government and certain provinces would be continuing their long-range policy of ensuring that French-speaking Canadians would have the same opportunity as their English-speaking compatriots to participate actively in the life of the country. The French policy of support for French-speaking Canada was likely to continue, though in a more restrained and reasonable fashion, accepting normal international practice, after De Gaulle had left the scene. Therefore Canada would, for many years, have a special relationship with France. No matter how cordial or frigid diplomatic relations might be at any given time, this particular relationship was likely to remain a constant in Canadian policy.[1]

DIPLOMATIC REPORTING

This activity is the fundamental business of an embassy, which must be the eyes and ears of the home government in the country where it is located. France under De Gaulle provided our Embassy with plenty of matters to report on. The General had large ambitions for his country and he played the role of "enfant terrible" very effectively, toward allies and enemies alike.

His attitude to NATO has been referred to previously. With the arrival of the Trudeau government in the late sixties, Canada was reconsidering its own commitment to that organization, and it was the Embassy view that De Gaulle would regard any Canadian withdrawal with indifference, except insofar as such a move would weaken Canada's diplomatic presence in Europe, and might encourage the U.S. to remove some of its own troops from the European continent. His suspicion of the European Common Market and his opposition to British membership—shared by a significant number of people in Britain—had implications for Canada, for it actually helped postpone the day when Canada would have to face up to the end of Commonwealth preferences that favoured the entry of Canadian exports into Britain. The General's policies toward the Soviet Union and Eastern Europe, the Middle East, and the American involvement in Vietnam are well known, and since Canada had commitments in all these areas, the Embassy continued to keep the federal government informed of them. The Embassy's work in the more strictly confined area of Franco-Canadian relations deserves fuller treatment.

TRADE RELATIONS

Though both France and Canada were major trading nations, trade was of little importance to their relationship because of the relative complementarity of their economies. There was a Trade Agreement, there were exchanges of business delegations and a Joint Economic Commission, but trade figures remained static. There were few Canadian investments in France at that time, while France, for reasons related largely to strategic reserves, had increased its investments sixfold in the previous ten years in oil and gas in Alberta and potash in Saskatchewan. A recent large private investment had been made by Michelin in Nova Scotia, but there was little investment in Quebec. Notwithstanding considerable efforts by France, Canada and Quebec, there was no change in this situation during the period covered by this book.

NUCLEAR COOPERATION AND SATELLITE COMMUNICATIONS

There had been close and continuing contact between French and Canadian nuclear scientists as a result of their working together during World War II, at the University of Montreal. These consultations continued, and indeed, this was one of the rare fields where despite the relations between the two countries, Canadian visitors were always welcome. Numerous forms of cooperation still existed, and at this time a new General Agreement was reached on proposed exchanges of information in which each country would share some of its most advanced technology. In addition, a sale of 150 kilograms of plutonium for use in French nuclear power stations, and subject to international safeguards, was approved by the Trudeau government in September 1968.

Satellite communication was developing rapidly, and Canada was in the vanguard with its Alouette program, to which two French technicians were attached. Furthermore, Canada was planning a domestic satellite system, one of the first in the world, that would ensure television programming across Canada in the two official languages. The French, for their part, were concentrating on the construction of a launcher in French Guiana that could play a key part in the evolving European Space Program.

This seemed to be a promising area for the development of cooperation between France, the government of Canada and the government of Quebec. Unfortunately, politicians with different agendas were to create roadblocks before such cooperation would be achieved. When Premier Johnson had visited De Gaulle in 1966 they had spoken of future cooperation, more specifically with regard to the Symphonie project. Both France and Quebec knew full well that in Canada communications was a field of mixed jurisdiction, and that any such arrangement would require Ottawa's participation or at least consent. Quebec's motive in having this field mentioned was to show that constitutionally, it could have discussions with foreign countries not only about matters of exclusive jurisdiction, such as education, but also about areas of mixed jurisdiction. Quebec seemed to be more interested in making constitutional points than in participating in the development of a Canada-wide bilingual satellite system.

In spite of political conflicts the Canadian and French communications technicians continued to keep in touch. On both sides it was known that Symphonie was an experimental project with many teething problems. It had originally been conceived as a joint undertaking of France and West Germany and the Germans had made it clear that their continued participation depended on Canadian assent. They had no desire to be involved in one of De Gaulle's battles with Ottawa. The U.S. also took the position that it would not launch Symphonie without Canadian approval. In the midst of this confusion, Canada informed France that it was interested in participating in the Symphonie project, as being consistent with its more general interest in some form of cooperation in the European Space Program. The issue wound its way along an intricate course and produced a major incident early in 1969 (see Chapter 9). Finally, in 1973, a small ceremony took place including representatives from France, Canada and Quebec to celebrate the first experimental transmission by satellite between France and Canada; the topic was a discussion between two groups of cardiologists concerning their treatment methods. Today TV 5, the station for La Francophonie, is regularly received in Canada.

Throughout the developments in these complex areas of nuclear cooperation and satellite communication, the Paris Embassy played a dual role. The evolution of France's programs and the way in which they might fit developments in Canada were the subject of regular reporting by the Scientific Counsellor at the Embassy, who also arranged the programs for the many visitors in these fields. In addition, the Embassy acted where necessary as a facilitator for the various negotiations between the French and Canadian scientific communities.

CONTACTS WITH PROVINCES

Those provinces with important French-speaking minorities, particularly New Brunswick, Ontario and Manitoba, were already engaged in widening the educational facilities of their Francophone citizens and hoped to participate in the activities of La Francophonie and in the meetings of Francophone Ministers of Education, if and when invited. Civil servants from these provinces were in contact with French educational authorities. The Embassy, however, had experiences with Ontario and British Columbia at a different level, which give some indication of English-Canadian attitudes toward France at that time.

In the spring of 1968 I received an informal visit from the Ontario Agent General in London. He informed me that there was a distinct possibility that Ontario would open an office in Paris. Apparently the province had been left some property in Paris that could be adapted to serve as offices. He said that Toronto recognized the political need for such a move, but some members of the government were unconvinced that there were sufficient commercial and financial incentives.

The Embassy strongly encouraged this Ontario initiative but told the Agent General that status could pose a problem. If Ontario wanted a commercial office only there would be difficulties, as no other foreign federal country had such an office in France at that time. If the province wanted a small Delegation General to deal with education and culture as well as commercial matters, that would be easier. The federal government could follow the procedure that had been used to secure Delegation General status for Quebec in 1963. France had made no advance commitment to accept other provincial offices, but while the response might be slow, we believed it would be difficult for France to refuse. Ontario had the largest French-speaking minority outside Quebec; it was engaged increasingly in educational exchanges with France and was creating, very gradually, a network of French-speaking schools in the province.

We had further discussions, one with an Ontario cabinet minister who visited that autumn, and were left with the impression that he would be recommending the opening of a small Delegation General. Nothing more was heard, though I learnt unofficially that the whole idea had been turned down for reasons related to the provincial political scene. My own guess was that the opposition came from within Premier Robarts' own Cabinet.

The following year, a friend who was an Ontario cabinet minister, led a business delegation to Paris. At the same time my old chief from London days, George Drew, was in town, so we invited both of them with their wives for drinks. I told them the story of the aborted Ontario mission in Paris and how much I regretted, as a Canadian, that Ontario had not seen fit to press for representation in Paris at this difficult time in our history. Reactions were interesting. My friend reeled off a variety of electoral reasons to explain why such a move would have been unwise. George Drew totally disagreed, believing that Ontario had missed an opportunity to contribute to Canadian unity. This was an interesting example of the difference between two provincial politicians, the one seeing pressures at a local level, and the other, judging them in the light of federal and foreign experience. Since then, Ontario has both opened and closed a Delegation General in Paris.

There was another incident, originating in British Columbia. In 1969, the Premier of that province, the late W.A.C. Bennett, accompanied by two of his friends, embarked on a private visit to a number of European countries to seek out new sources of investment. For his visit to France he had dealt with the French Consul General in Vancouver, who promised him a full program and a meeting with the Secretary of State for Foreign Affairs, De Lipkowski. By the time Ottawa learnt of this trip, the Premier had already left Canada. At that time there was extreme nervousness in Ottawa about a forthcoming visit of De Lipkowski, who was going to Quebec but had turned down an invitation to Ottawa (see Chapter 13). Bennett was to see him a week before his departure. A somewhat panicky message was sent from Ottawa to the Premier in Germany, warning him that De Lipkowski might try and turn his private visit into an official one. The purpose of the message was to ensure that the Premier did not fall into a trap by seeming to be on good terms with De Lipkowski when a confrontation with the federal government was about to take place. Premier Bennett did not appreciate having his ability to act and speak on behalf of Canada called into question.

When he arrived in Paris he was thoroughly disgruntled with the "Feds" and looking forward to the program promised by the French. Fortunately, those promising a full visit and those responsible for a program never consulted each other, much less the Canadian Embassy. He was met at the airport by our Ambassador and a tardy junior protocol official, and it quickly transpired that there was no program for the Premier. We managed to salvage most of the visit and the Premier met a wide selection of businessmen at lunches given by De Lipkowski and the Embassy. In the end, the British Columbia party were no longer angry with Ottawa, but were irritated at the way they had been treated by the French. After listening to De Lipkowski, Premier Bennett told us he was convinced that there was a plot in official French circles to destroy Canadian unity. Thus another Canadian public figure learned something of French intentions toward Canada from personal experience, after having refused to listen to advice from Ottawa.

VISITS

Visits are a recognized form of diplomatic intercourse and in normal times we had a regular procession of ministers, parliamentarians, members of delegations and other dignitaries through Paris. Since De Gaulle's speech in Montreal there had been only one visit of a cabinet minister in over a year, while Quebec visitors poured in continually. There was little contact between France and the rest of Canada, a situation that would remain unchanged until De Gaulle left the scene. Three visits from that period that come to mind give the flavour of our relations at the time.

The 50th Anniversary of the End of World War I
De Gaulle had the idea that few in France remembered the First World War, in which France with her Allies had been victorious. A grand national celebration would teach the young something of the sacrifices of their grandfathers and would help to offset the many celebrations taking place in France commemorating events during the Second World War, when France had been conquered, occupied, divided and liberated. It seemed a good idea at the time, but by November 11, 1968 the youth of France had already rebelled against what they considered to be an outdated system.

In any case, the celebrations went ahead, culminating in a parade in which military detachments from Allied countries of the First World War marched with the French Armed Forces. These detachments provided an interesting lesson in European history. The Italians and Romanians had been enemies of France in the Second World War. The Soviet detachment should not have been there, since it was Czarist Russia that had been France's ally and the Bolsheviks had made a separate peace. Tito's Yugoslavia represented Serbia, even though it was the actions of a Serbian terrorist that had started the War. The British empire had vanished and so, in addition to a detachment from Britain, there were also Canadian and ANZAC battalions. Finally, apart from little Belgium, invaded twice, the only Allies that had fought with France in both World Wars were "les Anglo-Saxons," from both sides of the Atlantic.

Canada sent a battalion of the Royal 22nd Regiment, two of the tallest members of the RCMP with enormous Canadian flags, who always managed to position themselves opposite General De Gaulle at each ceremony, and a delegation of 150 veterans. We entertained the whole group at the residence and the vets came marching in to "It's a Long Way to Tipperary," drank their two glasses (all that they were allowed), and marched out to "Mademoiselle from Armentières." I asked the brigadier general in charge how the visit had gone: "Oh, not bad, we lost only one man in Amiens, last seen with a prostitute." None of the vets was under seventy.

The Ministers of Agriculture
Since there were no federal ministers visiting France we had what we thought was a bright idea. We would invite a visiting Canadian minister

to the Organization for Economic Cooperation and Development [OECD] in Paris to have lunch with his French opposite number. We picked the Canadian Minister of Agriculture, because both countries were major food exporters, we were establishing, with the French, a quarantine station in Saint-Pierre and Miquelon for Charolais cattle being imported from France, and it seemed that agriculture was at that time a relatively innocuous subject. I had stupidly not taken into account the problem of language. When they came to my residence I realized that neither the Minister, who was from the West, nor any of his officials, spoke a word of French; not surprisingly, the French group did not speak English. I spent what seemed a very long lunch interpreting between the two ministers. My problem was that I knew nothing about agriculture.

Federal Members of Parliament
The House of Commons Committee on External Affairs and Defence was travelling to NATO countries in order to make recommendations about future Canadian relations and roles within the Alliance. In early 1969 they came to Paris and were received by De Lipkowski, presumably wearing a Canadian hat instead of his usual Quebec one. What was billed as a half-hour courtesy call turned into an hour and a half of give and take on Franco-Canadian relations. This was a fascinating and comforting experience for one who had been engaged in the day-to-day battle with the French for over a year. The atmosphere was at times strained but always correct, the positions taken were more than frank and it was the French-speaking parliamentarians who took it upon themselves to defend the Canadian cause.

De Lipkowski pretended that relations with Quebec and Canada were reasonably good despite a certain irritation shown by the Canadian government about specific cases. Certainly they were more important than with some other countries with whom France had relations. He repeated the usual litany about France's moral debt to those his country had abandoned. He then defended De Gaulle's visit as being designed to help defend French language and culture. The way the General had been received showed that there was a malaise: "Our cooperation with Quebec is a wonderful and great policy which we will not renounce." He totally failed to realize the effect his words would have on French-speaking MPs from Quebec elected to serve in Ottawa. This was not surprising, since he was meeting for the first time French-Canadian MPs who had a mandate that was national rather than provincial.

The Canadian MPs counter-attacked. No one was against greater French cooperation with French-speaking Canadians, indeed it was about time that something was done. But the methods used, putting Quebec first and dealing with other French Canadians under the terms of the Cultural Agreement with Ottawa, merely split French Canadians amongst themselves and caused a backlash from the English-speaking Canadians amongst whom they lived. French gestures menacing Canadian unity, such as support for separatism or a Quebec international personality, were unacceptable: France should deal with French Canada on the same basis throughout and not give Quebec preferential treatment.

When De Lipkowski replied that Quebec provincial members said something quite different, he was given a lesson on the realities of a federal state. The leader of the French-speaking MPs summed up as follows: "France must respect the point of view of French-speaking Canadians, often nationalist like himself, but who believe in the future of Canada and the possibility of English and French Canada being able to cohabit and cooperate for the common good."[2]

This was the first time that a French Minister had had to listen to the point of view of Canadian MPs of both official languages belonging to different political parties. He should have been impressed by their unanimity and warmth of their attachment to the idea of Canada. Unfortunately, we never noticed that this visit had the slightest effect on De Lipkowski.

THE CANADIAN PRESENCE IN FRANCE AND IN THE MEDIA

The Embassy found itself frozen out of most contacts with the Gaullist government and under sporadic attack from De Gaulle himself, but it had to keep in mind that France would remain important to Canada long after De Gaulle had departed. We therefore devised a policy of "Canadian Presence" in France to remind the French of our past common experiences in two World Wars and our presence as allies in NATO, to show that Canada was a modern industrial state with large primary resources and a major world trader, and that it was engaged in trying to give the French language and culture equal status with English. In carrying out this policy we were up against a strong rival in the Quebec Delegation, whose active and able Press Secretary, Gilles Loiselle—later to become a Mulroney Cabinet Minister—was given ready access to official circles and the French press.

Our objective was to try to give the Canadian point of view and describe the country as it really was, in order to achieve some balance in the contest for the minds of French opinion makers. This in itself was difficult enough but, in addition, we had to face the fact that the Department of External Affairs did not and would not understand the importance of cultural and press relations in foreign policy. They were not seen as a key area like pure foreign and economic policy. The French, on the other hand, understood full well that French culture and language were an integral part of foreign policy and the Cultural Directorate General of the Quai d'Orsay received an impressive budget.

At this time we had in Paris, as a consequence De Gaulle's visit, the largest Canadian press contingent in one foreign capital in our history, except for the journalists in London during the Second World War. There were about a dozen regular correspondents from newspapers and agencies and as many stringers. In addition there was the French press itself, only fitfully interested in Canadian Affairs, though *Le Monde* followed events regularly. Finally, Radio-télévision Française had a correspondent with separatist sympathies in Montreal. The main interest of the journalists was in the triangular relationship between Paris, Ottawa and Quebec, and the more discord there was among them, the more stories there were to be printed. At the Embassy, where we had no adequate guidance from Ottawa, we had little success in the early days in bringing balance and a sense of proportion into the public comment on the various crises that occurred, particularly as the French government and the Quebec Delegation had an interest in either exaggerating every event or interpreting it as best suited them.

We were also up against the "feedback phenomenon" because of the five or six hour time difference between Canada and France. A story breaking in Paris could reach Ottawa for Question Period in the House of Commons or the News Programs, ensuring a reaction from either Quebec or Ottawa or both on the same day. This would be in the Paris press the next morning, when we would learn of it for the first time. Similarly, a story starting in Canada would be read by us for the first time in the Paris morning press, or we would learn of it from a diplomatic colleague. It was rare for Ottawa to warn us in advance. A simple solution would have been to rent an Agence France-Presse ticker which would provide us with advance warning. For three years we tried to convince Ottawa of this, without result. This situation made it extremely difficult to deal with the Paris-based correspondents regarding any story, for they already had official reactions from their French and Quebec contacts.

With the arrival of the Trudeau government we finally received the services of a full-time professional Press Officer. He proved to be invaluable, for he had worked for Canadian Press for many years, had covered Quebec during the Duplessis years and was a convinced federalist. At last we had someone who could on his own initiative and in consultation with the appropriate officer act as Embassy spokesperson on any given event likely to interest the press. He cultivated the Canadian, Paris and the French provincial press corps, French TV and Radio, and specific stars in the Paris journalistic firmament. It was also he who convinced me that we were not using our resources adequately and that the various Canadian government departments and agencies represented in Paris (about a dozen) should be able to cooperate in establishing together a regular program on what we rather grandly called "The Canadian Presence in France."

Our purpose was to use all suitable public occasions, such as an exhibition of Canadian art, attendance at public conferences, or a Canadian stand at commercial fairs outside Paris, to present a picture of modern Canada from coast to coast to an audience which, because of Expo '67 and De Gaulle's "Vive le Québec libre" had an interest, if only an ephemeral one, in things Canadian. We were up against a series of stereotypes: a land of wind and snow and Indians, the song "Ma cabane au Canada," Maria Chapdelaine, a folkloric attitude to all the "cousins" in Canada, the Mounted Police, and so on. To accomplish our purpose we as good Canadians established a committee. It included the Trade Office for attendance at fairs; the National Film Board for films of Canadian life; immigration booths at our events to encourage the French to settle in Canada; the Cultural Section, to arrange our more intellectual and less commercial events; the Tourist Bureau, to encourage tourists to go to Canada; and the Canadian Exhibition Commission, to design and install our various displays. I had expected that in true bureaucratic fashion some agencies would object to the Embassy intruding into their work. The reaction was quite the contrary: they were pleased to be part of the overall Embassy effort and they acquired a better understanding of the concerns of senior management, for I always briefed them at our regular meetings on recent events in the Canadian-French relationship.

We had two main objectives in launching this initiative: to create in France an interest in and a better understanding of the whole of Canada; and to sponsor, or participate in, events that required reporting by at least the Canadian press, thus providing our own "feedback" to Canada. I remember presiding over at least ten Canada Days in different parts of

France, opening the Canadian stand at the local fair, visiting the prefect and the mayor, and giving interviews on the local television station. In retrospect I believe we had some limited effect; it certainly gave us the impression that we were standing up for the country during a difficult period in its history.

THE CANADIAN CULTURAL CENTRE

Another important new Canadian presence in Paris was provided by the decision of the government to create a Canadian Cultural Centre, to provide a meeting place, exhibition space and a resource base for the Canadian intellectual and artistic colony of both languages living in Paris and for visitors from Canada. The Centre caused us many problems. The house had been bought with the proprietor allowed to continue living on the top floor until her death. Though she was ninety-six she proved to be long-lived and we did not have the use of one floor. A more serious difficulty was the fact that External Affairs had never had experience with a cultural centre and sent a unilingual architect who, being completely at a loss, took to drink.

The lack of adequate professional assistance from Ottawa became such an acute problem that I stopped all work on the project until we should be given proper plans and personnel. This caused outrage in Ottawa, as it was meant to do, and brought down upon us a furious Undersecretary Marcel Cadieux. I sent him to the site with my two colleagues whose talent and hard work had been responsible for whatever progress we had made. He grasped the situation and we soon had a new team from Ottawa. The opening of the Cultural Centre in the spring of 1970 was to provide the occasion for a marked improvement in relations between France and Canada (see Chapter 16).

CONSULAR SERVICES

Canadian tourists continued to come to France in large numbers and lose their passports and money or break French law and end up in jail. We were expected, as always, to look after such cases quickly and with understanding, for the government had no wish to see stories in the media reporting that the Embassy was ignoring the plight of Canadians, particularly those who were French-speaking, in De Gaulle's France. Consular work was full of surprises. One day the Consular Officer phoned me to say that there was an old gentleman who had arrived with a pile of legal documents requiring consular authentication. He claimed he was the Duke of Windsor and he was selling a ranch near Lethbridge. Did I think this was a likely story? I did, and had the Duke escorted to my office. He was selling the ranch because the Duchess had said that the money was needed. It had been given to him by the people of Canada. I had a difficult half hour with him because he was like an empty shell and conversation did not flow. His memories of Canada were dim but he had been impressed by a former Mayor of Montreal, Médéric Martin. Oddly enough, his brother and sister-in-law had been impressed by another charismatic nationalist Mayor of Montreal, Camillien Houde, when they had visited Canada in 1939.

NOTES

1. Embassy Paris Telegram to Ottawa, no. 3526, September 19, 1968.
2. Embassy Paris Telegram to Ottawa, no. 831, March 21, 1969.

8

AN EXCHANGE OF AMBASSADORS

FROM THE POINT OF VIEW of Franco-Canadian relations, 1968 had not been a good year; it had been marked by the definite setback in Gabon involving Quebec's search for an international personality, and by the Rossillon affair, in the course of which intemperate remarks had flown back and forth across the Atlantic. Meanwhile, the General proceeded toward his referendum on reform, as a consequence of the Events of May, but it was becoming more and more doubtful that he could accomplish his purpose, in view of his age and the absence of fresh new personalities in his government.

At home in Canada there were signs of some willingness to find a form of compromise between Ottawa and the new Quebec government, headed by Premier Bertrand, concerning the Meetings of the Francophone Ministers of Education. While the Trudeau government had so far contributed more noise than accomplishment to relations with France, there was no doubt about its strength of purpose and its refusal to budge on the principle that the federal government alone exercised sovereignty in international relations. The battle, as far as we could see, would continue in the coming year, but the field on which it was fought would be more even.

Jules Léger was to be replaced in early November by Paul Beaulieu, one of two Canadian Ambassadors accredited to the United Nations in New York. Léger's tour of duty at the Paris Embassy had been momentous and uniquely difficult. He had tried with some success to broaden the relations between Ottawa and Paris after the Pearson visit in 1964. He had worked hard at trying to convince the Gaullist government that the new bilingual and bicultural policies being put into place by the federal government were worth supporting to ensure the international future of the French language and culture. Unfortunately De Gaulle preferred the narrow and more ethnically nationalist tone, the same as his own, that he was hearing from Quebec. With the De Gaulle visit to Expo Léger's hopes collapsed and it became clear that the Head of the Embassy in Paris would, for the foreseeable future, be engaged in a holding operation aimed at limiting damage.

It was time for him to move on, and while he would have preferred to return to External Affairs, he was asked to serve as Undersecretary in the Department of State of Canada, now strengthened and headed by Gérard Pelletier. As a team they would have the mission of putting into practice Ottawa's good intentions toward French-speaking Canadians throughout Canada, who were to be afforded equal opportunities for the use and protection of their language and culture. Léger had often complained that Ottawa was too inclined to concentrate on the "legalisms" of international sovereignty; unless it developed and carried out programs to assist French-speaking Canadians, particularly those outside Quebec, "legalisms" would count for little. The policies he would have responsibility for implementing would involve a degree of French assistance, which should tend to make French policy toward Canada less exclusively focused on Quebec. He had therefore to some extent argued himself into a position where his experience and prestige could be put to use in a cause in which he strongly believed. As for those of us who worked at the Embassy, we would miss his experience and knowledge, which had made it a pleasure to work with him.

Before Léger left he paid one last visit to Couve De Murville. He put it to the French Prime Minister that, as he ended his mission, he had come to realize more and more that relations between the two countries were conditioned by the millions of French-speaking Canadians in Canada and that without their presence Canada for France would be another Australia. This fact created a special situation for both countries, which had to be taken into account in the elaboration of our respective policies, particularly at a time when these policies were just beginning to be put into effect. Couve agreed, and while Léger's argument might seem obvious or repetitious it could not be repeated often enough both to French and to Canadian politicians. Couve remained his cool and distant self throughout. As Léger reported, he would never stop De Gaulle from meddling in our affairs, but he would, where possible, exercise a pacifying influence. It was the most we could hope for at the time.

Paul Beaulieu duly arrived and presented his Letters of Credence to General De Gaulle on December 14, 1968. The ceremony was short—ten, instead of the normal twenty minutes—extremely chilly but correct.

In answer to the Ambassador's traditional remarks about hoping to improve relations between the two countries, De Gaulle replied that he also hoped for cooperation and that this was possible on practical questions and international relations where both countries had common interests.

De Gaulle then went on to say that his ideas on the actual system of government in Canada were well known, and on this subject he did not have the same view as the federal government. There existed a unique situation in Canada, thanks to the existence of a group of more than six million "French of Canada," and conditions were no longer the same as at the time of Confederation. An accommodation between the two groups was needed and he hoped that such an accommodation or formula would be developed in Canada. It was clear, and hardly surprising, that his views on Canada and the future of Quebec had not changed since his November 1967 press conference. We could therefore continue to expect disagreements and crises in our relations until he left the scene.

Great men are often capable of being small-minded: while indicating his dislike of Canada as it was to the new Ambassador, De Gaulle delivered a minor insult on the periphery of the ceremony. It was normal on these occasions for an official photograph to be taken of the General with the new Ambassador, and the press was allowed into the Elysée courtyard to take photographs after the presentation ceremony was over. This arrangement had been confirmed to us the day before by the Elysée, who also told us that it was no longer the custom for the General to provide the press with the text of his remarks during the ceremony. On the day, no official photograph was taken, and on the General's orders the press was refused entry into the courtyard. Meanwhile, the text of his remarks was given to the press, so we issued the text of the Ambassador's statement.

The press, particularly the Canadian reporters, blew this up into another incident, but Ottawa did not agree. The assessment of Undersecretary Cadieux was that the proceedings had been correct.[1] Ottawa was relatively satisfied that while the General had repeated the essentials of his thesis about Canada's future, he had not used the occasion to start a new confrontation by more categorical statements. By this time, our leaders were thankful for small mercies.

In the meantime, the new Ambassador entered upon his duties. I had been told by some colleagues who had served in previous posts with him that they had been surprised by his nomination, given the state of relations between Canada and France. When I met him I discovered a small gentle man possessed, as I would learn, of a profound culture and deeply interested in literature, but apparently not desirous of facing up to the situation in which he found himself. As time progressed it became clear that he had little stamina or energy and was content to take a passive approach to his position. He called on few diplomatic colleagues, French ministers or senior civil servants; he carried out instructions from Ottawa but that was all; and he seemed content to remain in his office. I undertook every morning, for the twenty-one months that he was with us, to brief him on past and future events and ask him for his views. In all that time I never had a conversation of substance. My colleagues had the same experience.

What were we to do? It troubled us that the French would take advantage of the situation, so we agreed that, on any occasion when the Ambassador was carrying out instructions from Ottawa, he would be accompanied by an appropriate officer. We would try to run the Embassy as a collective, but inevitably the greatest burden fell on the Ambassador's deputy: myself. This unsatisfactory situation must have worried the Ambassador as well but he seemed incapable of breaking out of his passivity and eventually his health suffered. I was fortunate in my colleagues, who provided full support, but our morale was inevitably affected as we continued our attempts to deal with our already difficult relations with the Quai D'Orsay and the Quebec Delegation.

NOTE

1. Memorandum from Marcel Cadieux to Secretary of State for External Affairs, December 17, 1968.

9

JEAN-GUY CARDINAL IN PARIS:
SPACE COMMUNICATIONS

DE GAULLE STARTED off 1969 with a New Year's Message which listed a number of international problems including "the free conduct of their own national life by the French people of Canada." This was followed by the visit to Paris, in January, of a major delegation from Quebec led by Jean-Guy Cardinal in his capacity as Deputy Premier and Minister of Education, and including Jean-Paul Beaudry, Minister of Industry and Commerce, and the ubiquitous Claude Morin.

For De Gaulle and for Quebec this visit was a second best. Since De Gaulle's appearance in Quebec in 1967 there had been an outstanding invitation to Premier Johnson that the latter had postponed for health and political reasons, and now Johnson was dead. The invitation had been extended to the new Quebec Premier by Couve De Murville during his attendance at Johnson's funeral, but Bertrand too had a heart problem, and could not travel to Paris. Meanwhile it was becoming embarrassing for Quebec that, after the series of agreements and the parade of ministers and civil servants through Paris, there had been no meeting at the top level for a year and a half. Cardinal was travelling to Paris to compensate for the inability of the present and former premiers to follow up on the standing invitation. He was coming to Paris not only as the second man in the Quebec government but also, in his own eyes and in those of the Gaullists, as the person most likely to be the next premier of Quebec. His arrival was somewhat spoilt by the fact that in the previous week the exclusive character of Quebec's attendance at meetings of the Francophone Ministers of Education, epitomized by Cardinal's own presence in Gabon, had been the subject of a compromise between the federal government and Quebec, permitting the attendance of a Canadian delegation at the next meeting, to be held in Kinshasa, the capital of Zaire (see Chapter 10).

We expected from this visit the usual remarks by De Gaulle on the future of Canada and the highest visibility for the Quebec delegation. This would just have to be lived through, but there was one area of substance where we expected some form of cooperative arrangement, namely space communications. This area of mixed jurisdiction was closely linked with telecommunications, which was a federal government responsibility and the object of a well-developed national program. For these reasons, whatever might be agreed between Paris and Quebec would be unacceptable to Ottawa unless the federal government had been adequately consulted and had accepted the proposals put forward.

We had been telling the French this every time the possibility of a visit by a Quebec Premier had surfaced during the previous year. In the weeks before the Cardinal trip we were instructed to go to the Quai D'Orsay on three separate occasions. On December 20, 1968 I saw Jurgensen to say that Ottawa understood that there might be an Exchange of Letters on space communications and if so, I was under instructions to say that the Canadian government expected to be informed of the facts and consulted in advance on the nature of any agreement. Jurgensen said that there was a 50-50 chance of an Exchange of Letters—we learnt later that the text had been ready for four months—and that he would refer the Canadian request to his authorities. I saw him again on January 3, when he told me that he was in a position to officially notify me that discussions on space communications would take place during the Cardinal visit but that there would be no prior consultations.

Our assessment at the Embassy was that Quebec had told the French that they did not wish them to consult Ottawa before the Cardinal visit. There would be some form of equivocal arrangement announced during the visit, based on mutual and general commitments which would leave the appearance of new steps forward in space communications, but which would not be an intergovernmental agreement because of the mixed jurisdiction. This would allow France to be seen as continuing to cooperate with Quebec, while cooperation with Canada could take place under the wing of the Franco-Canadian Mixed Commission, due to meet in Paris the following month. The arrangement would suit the French, since they could claim that in space communications France was consulting with both Canadian parties separately but within the terms of the Franco-Canadian Cultural Agreement of 1965. They would ignore the fact that there had been no prior consultation with Canada, as called for in the Agreement and requested on numerous occasions before Cardinal's arrival.

What was disregarded in this complicated ploy was the manner of Quebec's cooperation with Ottawa, which had the competence, the resources, and part of the jurisdiction. Quebec still seemed to be more interested in the *form* of its cooperation with France than in actual collaboration that could eventually lead to Franco-Canadian space communications.

When Premier Bertrand announced the Cardinal trip, we were instructed once again to raise the whole matter in great detail with Alphand, the Secretary General at the Quai. The Ambassador saw Alphand, who took notes, said he was not *au courant* (highly unlikely in view of my previous conversations with Jurgensen) and would report to his Minister. This was a relatively normal reaction from Alphand, who disliked dealing with the never-ending parochial disputes between France and Canada, which had nothing to do with foreign policy and were decided not by his Foreign Minister but by De Gaulle.

The next event was my visit to the Economic Director of the Quai, who had called me in to receive an Aide-Mémoire constituting the French reply to the Canadian Aide-Mémoire on Space Research given to Debré by Sharp the previous October in New York. As we had anticipated, the French wished to show that they were also interested in cooperating with the federal government in space research before Cardinal arrived in town and there were the inevitable reactions to his visit. The Economic Director confirmed to me that an agreement would be signed by Quebec and France and that the French would give us the text after the signature. There would be two principal agreements: the first, to explore the possibility of a France-Quebec communications satellite, and the second, to send some Quebec technicians to France to familiarize themselves with communication satellite technology. [1]

And so Cardinal arrived in Paris, to be clasped in the close embrace of General De Gaulle. There were four visits to the Elysée Palace in five days, meetings with the Prime Minister and other ministers and so forth, but when it came to substance there appeared to be a certain caution on both sides that contrasted with the warmth of the reception. The Canadian press, as was its wont, concentrated on appearances, making comparisons with the receptions given to heads of state of sovereign countries and noting that the Canadian Embassy was ignored throughout the visit. The French press, generally speaking, did not report on the visit at all.

Ottawa played down the protocol aspects of the visit, though the Prime Minister could not resist making some remarks. In answer to a question from Diefenbaker in the House of Commons, he pointed out that when it was a matter of substance, such as the Gabon affair, Canada had vigorously protested, but that when it came to social events to which the Canadian Ambassador might or might not be invited, "it was the sovereign right of the French Government to give dinners to whom they wanted, and our Ambassador knows of other places in Paris where he can get a good meal."[2] This remark caused some hilarity in Paris, for the food at the Elysée under De Gaulle was notoriously second-rate.

The unofficial line from the Elysée came from Broussine, who played up what the General considered to be the two most important elements of the visit. The first was the establishment of direct links between Old France and New France, Paris and Quebec. This was not a new idea since both Quebec, and Ottawa within the limits of the Canadian constitution, had been trying to realize it for some years. The second was the agreement reached on the joint venture to construct and launch a communications satellite—the writer ignored the fact that, since Canada had the expertise and the French had just indicated a desire to cooperate with Canada, any Franco-Quebec satellite was unlikely to materialize without Canadian participation. Broussine went on to flatter Cardinal as "a man of exceptional worth who would play a key role in the evolution of French Canada." Cardinal was to disappear from the political scene within two years. Trudeau was dismissed as a "French-Canadian known for his hostility to the affirmation of the French Fact in North America. French Canadians only voted for him because he was French-Canadian not because of his ideas."[3] Trudeau would be Prime Minister for another fifteen years.

There were three sets of letters exchanged between France and Quebec dealing with satellite communication, investment and the University of Montreal. The Embassy's assessment of the substance of these letters was that they were remarkable only in that they dealt with matters already underway. The agreement to establish a study for an eventual Franco-Quebec communications satellite was not very conclusive and had to be viewed in conjunction with the French offer to cooperate with Canada in this same area under the Franco-Canadian Mixed Commission. This ambivalence had to be balanced by the refusal of the French to consult Canada on the subject before the Cardinal visit and the fact that they had given us the text after it had been signed between Paris and Quebec. This action would require an official reaction from the federal government. The Letter on Investments perfected a mechanism that already existed. And the continuing problem was that at that time French investment was very small in Quebec and much larger in the rest of Canada. The third

Letter relating to the University of Montreal was not strictly necessary, since it fell within an already existing agreement on education.

The communiqué announcing the results of the visit tried to give the impression of more progress than had actually occurred. For example, the reference to encouraging emigration to Quebec, another mixed jurisdiction, would probably receive little impetus, for the federal government had also tried to do the same thing and had been told that France was more interested in increasing the population of France than in encouraging emigration, even to New France. Interestingly, there were no invitations to specific French ministers to go to Quebec, such as had occurred after the De Gaulle visit. All in all, the Cardinal visit had changed little in the relationships between the three parties; indeed, France and Quebec showed some caution. For example, Cardinal, when he returned to Quebec, announced that the Letters signed in Paris were not intended to constitute inter-governmental agreements. In any case a much more important battle was on the horizon, in which France could greatly assist Quebec: the issue was the creation of La Francophonie and Quebec's international status within that organization.

Once the Letters between France and Quebec had been examined in Ottawa, Mitchell Sharp made a statement in the House of Commons, on January 31, 1969 on behalf of the government. The part of his statement dealing with space communications read as follows:

I should reiterate that the Canadian Government has adopted, in the matter of space communications, a very active policy consistent with its exclusive responsibilities for telecommunications and with the interests of the country, including those of Quebec and of French Canadians throughout the land.... We have established ourselves as pioneers in space research and have had exchanges with a number of countries, France included.... What is required in my view is a willingness to approach in a generally co-operative spirit the various projects contemplated where the Canadian Government has an essential role to play.... In this instance it seems to me that as the participation of the Federal Government will be required in any satellite scheme and therefore consultations will of necessity be involved it would have been preferable for the Quebec Government to be willing to take into its confidence the Government of the country, and to disclose its intentions, before making them known and including them in letters of intent to the government of another country.

We were subsequently asked to give the official comments of the federal government on the Exchanges of Letters to Secretary General Alphand. The purpose, once again, was to state clearly the juridical position of the federal government so as to ensure that such exchanges could not be considered as a precedent in the international domain:

Ottawa found it difficult to understand the intentions of France when ingenuity was exercised to multiply the confusion in our relations by such means as absence of consultation, forms of texts with Quebec that added nothing to agreements already in existence, signature of these texts which were then announced as not being agreements etc. All this could be interpreted as being an intention on the part of France to persuade Quebec to take international initiatives such as the signing of a treaty that could only be undertaken by an independent state. Such a policy was not only against international law, but also incomprehensible in terms of the interests of Quebec, Canada and French as an international language and culture.[4]

The Ambassador saw Alphand on February 21 to carry out his instructions. Alphand once again confined himself to the now traditional generalities. As an example, "France wanted to help Quebec without interfering in Canadian affairs." Since at Quebec's request France was acting outside the original Franco-Canadian Cultural Agreement by dealing directly with Quebec on matters of mixed jurisdiction, France was automatically interfering in Canadian affairs. This then was the official close to the Cardinal visit.

In the past six weeks we had had three disagreeable events relating directly to Franco-Canadian relations, namely, the presentation of Ambassador Beaulieu's Letters of Credence, the Cardinal visit, and the Kinshasa Conference of Francophone Ministers of Education (see Chapter 10). It was time for me to review the situation with Saint-Légier at the Elysée. I mentioned the three events to him and asked whether we were entering a more active phase in French policy toward Canada. Saint-Légier did not think so; circumstances had dictated recent events, since the three subjects had come up within the same time frame. That being the case, it was natural for General De Gaulle to use these occasions to express once again his well-known attitude toward Quebec and Canada.

Saint-Légier thought the Cardinal visit had not broken any new ground and had passed off relatively well in the circumstances. With regard to the communications satellite, the Exchange of Letters was only about a study and therefore, as yet, had no practical consequences. For this reason Saint-Légier pretended that there was no conflict with federal jurisdiction and therefore no need to consult Ottawa. The French had found their Quebec visitors concerned by the fact that the Union Nationale leadership question had not been settled and that they were entering a phase that could lead to a relatively early election. Hence Cardinal had been anxious to avoid giving the impression that his delegation was engaged in anything other than normal consultations in areas which Quebec considered within its own jurisdiction.

Saint-Légier thought our relations would continue to be much the same as in 1968—hardly a consoling thought—and when occasions presented themselves the General would again express his views, which could lead to further public differences. This of itself did not represent a change in the situation which had existed since De Gaulle's return from Canada, but meanwhile, practical cooperation with Canada and Quebec would continue. This would be the last time I would see Saint-Légier in his capacity as Political Counsellor to De Gaulle, for he was to depart with the General two months later. I would miss his courtesy and the ingenuity he brought to trying to convince me that Franco-Canadian relations were not as bad as they really were. He was a good diplomat in the traditional mould.

NOTES

1. Embassy Paris Telegram to Ottawa, no. 185, January 21, 1969.
2. House of Commons, *Debates*, 4706, January 23, 1969.
3. Embassy Paris Telegram to Ottawa, no. 225, January 24, 1969.
4. Ottawa Telegram to Embassy Paris, S 153, February 14, 1969.

10

HOSTILITIES IN AFRICA,
ROUND TWO

TWO INTERNATIONAL francophone meetings were due to take place in early 1969. The first, bringing together the Francophone Ministers of Education, was to be in Kinshasa, the capital of Zaire. It was at the previous annual meeting in Gabon that Ottawa had lost the first round of its dispute with Quebec over the province's claim to have international status for matters within its own domestic jurisdiction. The other meeting was to be held in Niamey, the capital of Niger, whose President Diori had been given a mandate by his fellow African presidents to organize the founding conference of a new international body to be known as La Francophonie.

Having been successful in Gabon the *indépendantistes* in Quebec were now concentrating on the Niamey meeting, where they hoped to take a further step toward international status by making Quebec a full member of this new international organization. France was assisting Quebec in this objective.

Meanwhile, Ottawa had not been idle; it had commenced the implementation of an aid program for Francophone African countries, administered in French, that had been given impetus by the Chevrier Mission; it had posted a foreign service officer on a roving commission based in Africa, to put forward on a regular basis the Canadian thesis on international sovereignty, and to act as a conduit to and from key African presidents to Trudeau; and it had sent Paul Martin, now Government Leader in the Senate, on a specific mission to explain personally to the most influential African leaders the international aspects of the Canadian constitution.

THE KINSHASA CONFERENCE

In retrospect it appears that after the Gabon affair the French had assumed that the question of Quebec's participation, without a Canadian presence, at the regular Conferences of Francophone Ministers of Education had been resolved. They thought that a notification of the next meeting would go to Quebec because it had participated in the previous one, and apparently did not realize that Canada would not and could not accept such a situation. Apart from this, the political situation in Quebec and Ottawa had changed with the departure of Premier Johnson and the arrival of Prime Minister Trudeau. Also the French had not thought through the consequences of having, as host country, a former colony not of France but of Belgium. President Mobutu was less open to direct personal pressure from General De Gaulle than President Bongo of Gabon had been. That they had misjudged the situation became evident when they learned that Zaire had sent invitations to Ottawa and also to its former colonial power, Belgium.

On receiving the invitation Marc Lalonde, the principal Secretary to the Prime Minister, who was the Ottawa official most directly involved, immediately informed the four provinces concerned—Quebec, Ontario, New Brunswick and Manitoba—and commenced negotiations for the establishment of a single Canadian delegation. After many peregrinations, complicated by Premier Bertrand's heart condition and a split within the Union Nationale government, a temporary agreement was reached whereby a Canadian delegation, co-chaired by Premier Robichaud of New Brunswick and Jean-Marie Morin, the junior Minister of Education in Quebec, would attend the conference. At the table each part of the delegation was identified by a sign that included the the word "Canada" followed by the name of the specific province, while a larger "Canada" sign was placed in front of all these signs. In addition, there were federal officials in attendance, including Lalonde, to ensure that there was no backsliding. This enormous and complex delegation must have been regarded with a mixture of awe and hilarity by the Africans, themselves no strangers to the problems created by tribal differences.

When they heard of the invitation to Ottawa Claude Morin and his coterie in Quebec were upset and asked their French friends to put pressure on Zaire to send a separate invitation to Quebec, alleging that Ottawa had not informed Quebec of the invitation. This allegation was quite untrue, for Lalonde had already started negotiations for a Canadian delegation including Quebec and the other provinces on the basis of the invitation. The French Ambassador in Kinshasa, who must have been in some disgrace for not having foreseen the original invitation to Ottawa, carried out his instructions with fevered enthusiasm. The Zairois, not wishing to create further trouble with France, sent a late invitation to Quebec, offering as justification that the province was a former partici-pant and so had not been invited. Despite all this the conference passed off reasonably well, though the main "Canada" sign was removed by a zealous French official and the French Ambassador, who led the French delegation, was extraordinarily rude to Premier Robichaud. I raised this later with Saint-Légier at the Elysée, saying that it was unfortunate that the leader of the French delegation had been unable to display the most elementary courtesies to Premier Robichaud, who was both a Franco-phone and the premier of a province with a large francophone population. He changed the subject.

The precedent of an international Canadian delegation, dealing with education but based on provincial representation that included Quebec, was an important step forward. There were no illusions on the federal side that France would abstain from efforts to redress the balance in Quebec's favour. Despite the fact that Paris had always said that it would accept any arrangement on which Ottawa and Quebec might agree, there was now great irritation amongst the French with all concerned in the new state of affairs, which was therefore not likely to be accepted.

To temper any French reaction, I received instructions before the Cardinal visit to see Jurgensen and ask for an explanation of the behav-iour of the French Ambassador in Kinshasa. I put four questions to my interlocutor: 1) Did the French Ambassador intervene with the govern-ment of Zaire to demand a separate invitation to the Conference for Quebec, as had been alleged by the Zaire authorities in a diplomatic note to Canada? 2) If yes, did he act on instructions? 3) If so, did that mean that the French government did not approve of agreements reached between Ottawa and Quebec, contrary to what had been asserted in the past? 4) If he did not act on instructions, might we assume that his supe-riors would take appropriate measures to ensure that there was no repeti-tion of such action?[1]

I had seen and was to see Jurgensen many times, but never was I to find him so uncomfortable and defensive as on this occasion. His reply to me was diffuse: "The Zairois, without consultation, had invited two new parties to the Conference, namely Ottawa and Brussels. The French were displeased at this discourtesy and disturbed that a previous participant, Quebec, had not been invited. The French Ambassador had therefore reminded the Zairois that all participants at Libreville were expected to be invited by the host country to Kinshasa and Quebec had not received an invitation." I expressed surprise that the French had seen fit to intervene with a third party regarding an invitation to a Canadian province to attend an international conference. This brought the usual reply that education was a matter of provincial jurisdiction, and my response that it was not for the French government to interpret the Canadian constitution. Jurgensen then wondered why we were so unhappy, since the Kinshasa Meeting was an important step forward from the point of view of Ottawa. I concluded the meeting by stating that the arrangements at Kinshasa represented an agreement between Canadians, a fact I hoped the French government would take into account when convening the follow-up conference, due to take place in Paris in April.

This confrontation had been rather fun, since it was rare for us to catch the French out and put them on the defensive. That this had been possible was due to the compromise agreement between Ottawa and Quebec but, as the Embassy informed Ottawa, we need not expect any change in French policy. Our guess for the follow-up conference was that France would send an invitation or a notification to Quebec and none to Ottawa, but that if an agreed federal-provincial Canadian delegation turned up for the Paris Meeting, the French would reluctantly have to accept the *fait accompli*.

THE FIRST NIAMEY CONFERENCE

President Diori of Niger was having his difficulties in organizing what was to be the first Conference of Partially or Entirely French-Speaking Countries (La Francophonie). This conference was to name a Provisional Secretary General who, together with Diori, would draft the constitution of a small multilateral aid office, better known as the Agence Francophone. This document would be discussed and confirmed at a second conference in Niamey the following year. Diori faced many problems, the most difficult being that there could not be a Francophonie without France, but the French were most reluctant to encourage and support financially an organization which would partially multilateralize their bilateral relations with former colonies and their related aid programs. In addition, such an organization would bring on the scene more partially French-speaking countries (the Cameroons was already a member) such as Canada, Belgium and Switzerland. This meant, insofar as Canada was concerned, the importation into La Francophonie of the trilateral France-Canada-Quebec dispute about Quebec's status in international francophone institutions.

If plans for La Francophonie were to proceed, then France intended to control the requirements, finances and administration of the new Agence. This faced the Africans with a dilemma: they could not proceed without France, yet La Francophonie was designed to lessen their exclusive dependence on France by giving them some breathing space in international affairs. They wished to respect Canadian national unity, being all too conscious of the fragility of their own recently acquired independence. In addition, they had a direct interest in Canada's membership as it would give them some access to North American technology and know-how. But French pressure to support Quebec's international personality was difficult to resist. In President Diori, Canada was fortunate to have an African leader who, while having to compromise with the French, managed to limit his compromises to non-essentials while supporting the basic Canadian thesis that there could be only one representative of Canada in international affairs.

The struggle to create La Francophonie, and the later evolution of the organization, would be long and complex, and much of it is beyond the scope of this volume. The purpose here is to concentrate on those aspects that affected relations between Canada and France (see Chapter 15). At the outset both Canada and President Diori faced a basic problem, in that most of the ideas and documentation for the Niamey Conference had come from the fertile mind of none other than Philippe Rossillon. This material was written on the assumption that Quebec would attend the Conference alone and would become the sole Canadian member of the new international organization. This was of course unacceptable, and made it necessary to initiate negotiations for a single Canadian delegation between Ottawa, Quebec and the other provinces with important Francophone populations.

There was also the conundrum posed by invitations. Diori had been told by the French that there should be only one invitation addressed to Quebec, and that if this did not occur then Quebec could boycott the conference and, by implication, so could France. As a countermove against this pressure, Trudeau sent Diori a letter dated October 2, 1968 indicating the interest of all Canadian Francophones in La Francophonie, and the intention of the Canadian government to ensure that the appropriate provinces of Canada were represented at Niamey.

Diori had to find a compromise that would relieve him of both French and Canadian pressure. He therefore replied to Trudeau's letter on November 18, sending at the same time a copy of a letter he had written to Premier Bertrand. In his letter to Trudeau Diori expressed his confidence that the discussions with the provinces would result in Canadian representation in Niamey, but also take into account "the eminent place that Quebec would be offered at the Conference, and in a spirit of efficiency and to ensure no delays," he had informed Premier Bertrand in order to ensure Quebec's attendance at the Conference, and he understood this to conform with the intentions set out in Trudeau's letter of October.

This compromise satisfied none of the parties. Paris was upset because Ottawa had been invited; the *indépendantistes* in the Quebec government were upset because the province would not go to Niamey alone; and Ottawa was displeased because Quebec had received what amounted to an invitation. Diori had managed to leave responsibility for the formation of the Canadian delegation where it belonged, in Canada. His manoeuvre was impressive, given his dependence on France and the precedent created by Quebec's attendance at the Conference in Gabon. He gave an example of the pressure brought to bear on him when he told Paul Martin—during the latter's visit—what had transpired when he had last seen De Gaulle. He had told the General that he intended to invite Canada to the Niamey Conference, to which De Gaulle had replied that "if he had been in Diori's place he would not invite Canada but would rather have invited Quebec."

Negotiations now took place between Prime Minister Trudeau and Premier Bertrand and their two senior officials, Marc Lalonde and Julien Chouinard. For once Claude Morin was not involved. An agreement was reached for a Canadian delegation to be led by Gérard Pelletier, Secretary of State, with the Quebec part of the delegation to be headed by Marcel Masse, Minister of State. This delegation turned out to be something of a two-headed monster, but it created a precedent: for the first time, at a Francophone international conference, the Canadian delegation was to be led by a minister of the federal government. There was one condition to which Ottawa agreed with reluctance. If there was disagreement within the Canadian delegation on how to vote on a particular subject, then the whole delegation would abstain. In practice decisions at the Conference were reached by consensus, so the condition, on this occasion, remained without effect.

The Niamey Conference took place and the fact that the Canadian delegation had a federal minister at its head forced the French delegation to behave themselves in public. They were correct but distant, though they used their activists behind the scenes, such as Rossillon and Bernard Dorin, to promote Quebec's international status. The assessment of the

Canadian delegation was that Niamey had given impetus to the formation of the multilateral aid organization and provided the opportunity to reinforce the Canadian position in La Francophonie. The main substantive decision of the Conference was that President Diori and the new provisional Secretary General, Jean-Marc Léger, would be responsible for drafting proposals for the future activities of the aid organization (L'Agence de Coopération Culturelle et Technique).

Jean-Marc Léger was an odd choice and certainly not one greeted with any enthusiasm in Ottawa. He was an avowed Quebec separatist, and presumably Quebec and Paris believed they had "their man at the Agence." Léger, however, took his multilateral responsibilities seriously, for if the Agence was to see the light of day all potential members had to agree to its constitution, and that meant Ottawa as well as Quebec. He tried, not always successfully, to act as a responsible and neutral international civil servant.

This was the sole accomplishment of the first Niamey Conference, though its communiqué contained the useful statement that the Agence "would operate taking into account the sovereignty of its member states." Our view at the Embassy was that, considering this was the first step in the creation of an international organization with world-wide representation, whose main goals were to protect and to project French language and culture, it was remarkable how little interest was shown in the French media and amongst the general public in France. The French government had also been relatively silent because of its lack of enthusiasm for the whole idea and its failure to achieve its objectives. President Diori had resisted French pressures and Canada, including Quebec, rather than Quebec exclusive of Canada, was now an element in the Francophonie equation. The French, however, do not give up easily and we predicted continuing efforts by them to limit Canada's action in La Francophonie.

THE SINGULAR VOYAGE OF MARCEL MASSE

Marcel Masse, who had been a co-chairman of the Canadian delegation at Niamey, had ambitions to be next leader of the Union Nationale; this made him a rival to Cardinal, and like the latter he thought his position would be strengthened by a performance on the international Francophone stage. In Paris, on his way to Niamey, he had reneged, in the presence of the Canadian press, on the agreement between Trudeau and Bertrand on the structure of the delegation. When he reached Niamey he informed his fellow Canadians that the Ottawa-Quebec agreement did not apply and that they would have to recommence negotiations with him, and insisted on a separate Quebec delegation at the Conference. After tedious negotiations a compromise was reached, based on the same formula for seating as at Kinshasa. During the Conference Masse acted as if he was of, but not in, the Canadian delegation. As those who had to deal with Masse discovered, he had an immense need to occupy centre stage. While this characteristic could lead him into ill-considered public utterances, it could also be played upon to bring a negotiation to a satisfactory conclusion.

Masse passed through Paris again on his return and took the opportunity to meet with De Lipkowski, a kindred spirit, and to pay a call on Debré, the Foreign Minister, as well as General De Gaulle. Debré was also reported to have said, in answer to a press question about Quebec independence, that such a question was up to Quebec but that France would continue to help Quebec whatever it decided to do. Ottawa was most unhappy with this performance, coming as it did directly after the Cardinal visit. Once again I was sent to see Jurgensen to remind him that the act of having every Quebec minister received by the Foreign Minister gave the impression that France supported Quebec's international status. I was turned away with soft words; Jurgensen thought that Debré's remarks were in accord with previous French policy—indeed they were— and that Masse's calls on De Gaulle and Debré were short courtesy calls where nothing of substance was discussed. This was yet another example of Ottawa's policy of not letting any opportunity slip by without giving an official reminder of Canada's view on Quebec's claim to an international personality. And so Masse left Paris; but he would return.

FOLLOW-UP MEETING OF FRANCOPHONE MINISTERS OF EDUCATION

This meeting was due to take place in Paris in April 1969. Trudeau spoke to Premier Bertrand, suggesting that since it was a follow-up to Kinshasa the previous arrangements could apply. At the same time he wrote the Premier, asking him to ensure that the French understood there was agreement in Canada and that they should not act against it. He also took the opportunity to repeat in tough terms the Canadian position on Quebec's international personality. Bertrand agreed to these terms provided that Ottawa was invited. This little trick was inspired by the fact that the French had already informed Quebec, but not Ottawa, that the Conference was to be postponed until the autumn because of the forthcoming referendum in France. Trudeau pointed out in a reply to Bertrand that no invitation was necessary; the French themselves had said so the previous year and Canada had been a participant at the Kinshasa Meeting.

The Embassy then received excited instructions to raise the whole question with Prime Minister Couve De Murville on the basis of his discussions with Trudeau in Quebec City, bearing in mind that the French had told us last year that no invitation was required. We were also to inform Couve that Trudeau and Bertrand had agreed on the Kinshasa formula and that there would be one Canadian delegation.

To send such instructions in the last week before the Gaullist referendum on reform, when there was a good possibility that De Gaulle might lose and leave the political scene, seemed to us most unwise.[2] We told Ottawa that Couve's time was totally taken up with the referendum campaign and that, since we had just learnt that the Conference had been postponed, we had more time to make our views known. We doubted that we would be received by Couve and suggested that Trudeau send Couve a personal message which we could deliver, and which Couve was more likely to see (an example of a practical answer to Headquarters designed to turn away wrath). Ottawa reluctantly agreed but preferred an oral message. In the end, none of this mattered, since De Gaulle lost the referendum and left the political scene. When we next faced the problem of relations with France at the end of the year, it was with a different president and a new French government.

NOTES

1. Ottawa Telegram to Embassy Paris, S 89, January 16, 1969.
2. Embassy Paris Telegram to Ottawa, no. 1126, April 23, 1969.

11

DE GAULLE DEPARTS,
GAULLISM REMAINS

IN THE MONTHS BEFORE THE REFERENDUM that would decide whether De Gaulle would continue to rule France, there had been a slight enhancement in the presence of the federal government in Paris. This was due to the meeting in February 1969 of the Franco-Canadian Mixed Commission provided for by the Cultural Agreement, the opening of a major exhibition of Indian and Inuit Art and Artifacts at the Musée de l'Homme and the visit of two Cabinet Ministers and the Parliamentary Committee of Foreign Affairs and Defence (see pages 66-67).

The Mixed Commission was chaired by Jurgensen and André Bissonnette, an Assistant Undersecretary from External Affairs, with representatives from Ontario and New Brunswick. It took place in a professional atmosphere and was severely practical, discussing such matters as scholarships, youth, and scientific, cultural and artistic exchanges. This meeting had no major effect on our relations with France but it put back on the agenda a useful annual exercise which demonstrated that France's exchanges with Canada in these fields were of importance and that Canada was making substantial efforts to encourage French language and culture among French-speaking Canadians outside Quebec. It also permitted the French to show that they were cooperating with Canada for the benefit of all Canadians and not only those living in the province of Quebec.

The Indian and Inuit Exhibition was of an extremely high calibre, representing the united efforts of French and Canadian experts over a number of years. Since the Baroness Rothschild had been closely involved in the preparations, the exhibition received wide press coverage and favourable reviews. It was opened by Gérard Pelletier, Canada's Secretary of State, and André Malraux, France's Minister of Culture, and the opening turned out to be a major anthropological and artistic event. It was popular amongst the French, many of whom were still inclined to regard the natives of North America as romantically described by Chateaubriand in

Two dancers from the Blackfoot nation at the Musée de l'Homme, early 1969.

his tale *Atala*, published one hundred and fifty years previously. The Canadian government, for its part, had started to encourage artistic talent amongst the Indians and Inuit, but at that time the place of Canada's Native Peoples within Canadian society was by no means on the national agenda. Fortunately the Blackfoot Nation of Alberta made available some of their dancers, who were greatly appreciated.

The visits of Gérard Pelletier and Jean Chrétien, who came to talk primarily about Arctic transportation, provided opportunities to publicize what Canada was doing or intended to do to assist French language and culture throughout the country. It also allowed the ministers to question in public whether a highly centralized nation state implying the existence of a dominant ethnic majority was the appropriate political formula for a country such as Canada, and to explain the advantages, for the safeguard of the French Fact in North America, of a loose federal system which gave the provinces wide powers in education and culture.

In the last six months of De Gaulle's rule, while we continued to be preoccupied with the never-ending problems of the Quebec-Ottawa-Paris relationship, we were very aware that the environment in which our disputes took place could change dramatically if the General were not successful in his referendum campaign. Aged nearly seventy-nine he was once again engaged in his "last great task" of saving the French from themselves by trying to change the nature of their governance. He had already given them back their self-respect after the traumas of wartime occupation and decolonization and had provided a strong presidential system capable of surviving his departure. Now he intended to introduce participation in the workplace, decentralize local government, renew the educational system and reform the Senate. As he saw it, if he was successful then France would be ready to face the challenges of the next decade; if he was not he would leave power in a proper democratic manner and there was a successor in the wings.

To outside observers the referendum seemed to be the the last gamble of a former great statesman who had become an old man in a hurry. His own personal position, both as leader of France and as an international statesman, had been seriously weakened by the May Events. He had placed Prime Minister Pompidou, the man who had saved the regime in May, "in reserve," and replaced his government by a group of tired Gaullist barons. This uninspired assemblage was expected to modernize France under the guidance of an elderly president halfway through his second mandate. In addition, participation was anathema to employers and of little interest to the unions; decentralization would involve a long process of negotiation between Paris and local authorities (actually started in the 1980s under the Socialists); and educational reform was, and is, a never-ending source of dispute in France.

We followed the various events of the campaign: the break between De Gaulle and Pompidou, who in the eyes of most Gaullists was the natural successor; the lack of interest in the campaign, even in traditional Gaullist strongholds; and the deep uneasy sense within the country that De Gaulle's reforms could lead to a new and much more fundamental challenge to the established order than that of May 1968.

Even so, there remained a strong and unquestioning Gaullist base in France that feared chaos if he were no longer there and who were still influenced by his threat to leave power if the referendum failed. Until the last ten days the polls indicated that the result could go either way, but then a small majority appeared who clearly preferred the known solid and unspectacular government of a Pompidou to the gamble of De Gaulle's reforms. De Gaulle knew that he had lost some days before the vote. He emptied the Elysée Palace of all his papers and left it, never to return, on the Friday before the Sunday vote. He gave an envelope to his Prime Minister, Couve De Murville, to be opened on Sunday evening when the results were known. It read, "I cease to exercise my functions as President of the Republic. This decision takes effect today at midnight," signed: Charles De Gaulle.

My wife and I sat at home and watched the results on television, as did everybody else in France. When it became clear that the referendum was defeated and that De Gaulle would leave power we opened a bottle of champagne and sent a telegram to Gaby and Jules Léger, who we knew would be celebrating with friends in Ottawa. It is rare in the Canadian Foreign Service to be at a foreign posting when the disappearance of a leader has an important effect on Canada. It had now happened to me twice. First in Moscow, when Stalin died; that was, of course, an event of importance to the whole world, but for Canada the Soviet Union was a next door neighbour. Now came De Gaulle's departure, not as universal in effect, but of direct interest to France's European partners and most particularly to Canada.

The General's disappearance from the political scene lifted a great weight off our shoulders at the Embassy, and it became possible to envisage a day when a more normal relationship would be established between France and Canada. Whatever happened in the forthcoming Presidential election, we would no longer be dealing with a semi-mythical autocrat whose regular pronouncements on the future of Canada seemed charged with inevitability and tore at the fabric of national unity.

We thought at the time, in what proved to be a burst of euphoria, that provided we moved carefully and tested French intentions it might prove possible to engage in a dialogue with the new French administration. If, as seemed likely, Pompidou were to be elected the Gaullists would be still very much in power. The new president would have the task of navigating between the demands of those who would insist that there be no change in Gaullist dogma and the need to jettison some of those principles in order to achieve a more pragmatic approach to France's major problems and to establish himself as his own man. Pompidou had never expressed any views on Canada in public, though he had been prime minister during the Pearson visit in 1964 and at the time of the General's Canadian visit in 1967. Could he be persuaded to work toward better relations with Ottawa while still providing assistance to Quebec, or would France continue to treat the federal government and Quebec as two separate entities with all the inevitable clashes this would bring? Much would depend on the different forces to be represented in the new government he would form after the presidential election. He, at least, was much less personally engaged than the General over the future of Canada. Quebec was understandably concerned at the disappearance of De Gaulle and indeed, shortly after the election, Claude Morin spent two weeks in Paris touching base with all his Gaullist contacts.

There were still many in Canada and France, who despite De Gaulle's rediscovery of French-speaking North America, would have been quite willing to see a return to the style of the previous period when Franco-Canadian relations were primarily based on sentiment and the common experience of two World Wars. Such a return was, in my view, no longer possible, for despite his unique and displeasing methods, De Gaulle had given irrevocable impetus to contacts between France and French-speaking Canadians. There were, in addition to this, the bilingual and bicultural policies of the Trudeau government and the continuing search by the Union Nationale government in Quebec for an international personality. It was therefore clear that the "Canadian Question" would have its place, though not as important a place as under De Gaulle, on the agenda of the new government in Paris.

Meanwhile, it was essential during the seven weeks of the presidential election campaign, to keep our heads down and avoid any action that could be interpreted by our enemies in the French administration as Canadian interference in the French electoral process. It was this advice that the Embassy kept repeating to Ottawa. Initially, our efforts to prevent damage during this critical period were successful.

Politicians at home work to their own domestic agenda and are often surprised when their plans for foreign visits collide with the domestic agenda of the country they intend to visit. Messrs. Don Jameson, Minister of Transport, and Jean-Luc Pepin, Minister of Industry, Trade and Commerce, were due to attend the Paris Air Show, meet opposite numbers and, in Pepin's case, try to revive the Franco-Canadian Economic Committee. We had to point out that while they could attend the Air Show, there was little point in visiting Gaullist ministers who would be out of power the following week and that such visits would be difficult to explain to the resident Canadian press corps. They both came and wisely confined themselves to the business community. The next problem was the sudden arrival of former Prime Minister Pearson to attend a conference as part of his mission for the World Bank on problems of Third World development. The World Bank had planned for him to see a number of Gaullist ministers, some of whom had been directly involved in actions against Canada. Moreover, Pearson was for the ultra-Gaullists the man responsible for the General having to leave Canada in 1967. In order to avoid unnecessary press speculation we managed to convince Mr. Pearson to confine his calls to a courtesy visit to Debré as Foreign Minister, and both former prime ministers had a non-controversial discussion on Third World aid without any mention of the words Canada or Quebec. These are two examples of a regular task of an Embassy: damage control.

Our next effort proved ultimately to be a failure and it destroyed any chance there might have been of starting a dialogue with the new French government. What became known as the Laurent Affair began quietly enough, when we were informed that De Lipkowski, preoccupied by the presidential election, would not lead the French delegation to the annual meeting of the France-Quebec Permanent Cooperation Committee in Quebec City. He would be replaced by Pierre Laurent, a senior Gaullist civil servant who had recently been appointed Director General of Cultural, Scientific and Technical Relations at the Quai D'Orsay. We consulted Ottawa, where it was suggested that, since Laurent was new, he would also wish to visit his Embassy in Ottawa, and if so they could arrange for him to meet his opposite numbers in the federal civil service.

It was at this point that the bureaucrats on both sides of the Atlantic started to play games. The French now told us that Laurent was not leading the delegation, just accompanying it; he would be making an introductory visit to Quebec and therefore would not be going to his Embassy in Ottawa. We told Ottawa that, while this was quite unsatisfactory, we did not think that the middle of the election campaign was the moment to make a case of it. We could inform the French of our displeasure, reserve our position and pass the matter off in public as a routine visit.

Unfortunately (and the files do not explain why), the matter was now removed from the European Division, which had responsibility for relations with France, and transferred to the Cultural Division, and it became clear to us that the matter was now being handled at a senior level in External Affairs directly with Lalonde in the Prime Minister's Office. We next received a telegram complaining that it was not understood why Laurent wanted to avoid Ottawa on his first visit to Canada (despite the fact that the battle about French visits to Ottawa had been going on for nearly two years). This telegram went on to explain that there was to be a Union Nationale leadership convention in the same time period and such a visit would raise press questions. We were instructed to inform the Quai that if Laurent came he should visit Ottawa first and return to Ottawa after his visit to Quebec to explain what he had been doing. [1]

We attempted to change this provocative approach by pointing out that the main objective was to avoid an incident in this period of interregnum. By taking the attitude suggested by Ottawa, when De Gaulle's government was still in power and when it was likely that the new government would be strongly Gaullist, might forfeit the opportunity for a dialogue with the new French administration and leave ourselves open to charges that we had exercised pressure during the presidential election campaign. This would be used by our Gaullist opponents and their Quebec friends to ensure that there would be no change in France's policy toward Canada, and it would not be forgotten by Laurent, so that the work of the Mixed Commission would be affected. We warned Ottawa that this was not just another bout in the dispute about visits but the first test of our relations with the new government about to be elected. We could minimize the affair, while reserving our position, until after the formation of the new government, or we could follow our instructions, with the inevitable strong reactions on the part of the French, particularly Debré, the Foreign Minister, who would decide whether or not Laurent went to Canada and who would be, as a member of the new government, one of the most faithful representatives of Gaullist ideology. [2]

The reply we received claimed that the Gaullists were trying to establish a precedent during the interregnum that would bind the new government after the elections. This was turning on its head our argument that the French would regard our attitude toward Laurent as taking advantage of the French election. The Embassy was caught between two mildly paranoiac attitudes, each regarding the actions of the other entirely in terms of current domestic problems and showing little concern for relations between the two countries. We were instructed to tell the French that it would be courteous and politic if Laurent visited the capital, but Ottawa would not insist that he come before and after the meeting in Quebec.

I had the dubious pleasure of conveying this message in as non-controversial terms as possible to my regular sparring partner Jurgensen. It was not a pleasant meeting; suffice it to say that Jurgensen took the point about this being Laurent's first visit to Canada. He also said that, since Ottawa considered his visit to be a serious problem, he would discuss it with him and his Minister Debré.[3] The latter decided that Laurent would not go to Ottawa or to Quebec. Shortly after the election we received informal messages to the effect that Debré had been furious and was reported to have said "we will get our revenge later." Debré certainly passed on the story to his successor, who had De Lipkowski call in the Ambassador two weeks after the election to inform him of the unfavourable repercussions of the Laurent incident but to say that the new Minister did not want to escalate the matter and that the incident was considered closed. As we shall see, it became clear in the autumn that this was not the case.

Pompidou easily defeated his main opponent, Senator Poher, the President of the Senate, and formed his new government. Trudeau sent him a message of congratulations—there had been no message when De Gaulle left power—that spoke of the need for dialogue between the two countries, the progress that had been made in cooperation, and the Canadian desire to widen the areas of such cooperation.[4] He received a non-committal reply. Mitchell Sharp also sent a message to the new Foreign Minister, suggesting they resume the custom of regular meetings at NATO or the United Nations.

The new Prime Minister Chaban-Delmas had been kept outside government by De Gaulle and appointed to be President of the National Assembly. He had not therefore been involved in the "Canadian Affair." More importantly, the new Foreign Minister Maurice Schumann would bring greater flexibility, though his Gaullist credentials could not be in doubt since he had been the General's spokesperson in London during the War. We had had dealings with him on the sale of plutonium and the agreement between the Canadian and French nuclear energy authorities. He preferred to be pleasant and not pick fights, but unfortunately his two Secretaries of State, Bourges and De Lipkowski, had been kept on: the first had caused us problems in La Francophonie and the second was in charge of the Quebec file. Foccart and his African network were also maintained. Collectively however, the new government, which had a number of centrists in it, should have proved less inclined to accept regular crises with Canada.

It was a remarkable fact that during the election campaign there had not been a single mention of Canada or Quebec by any candidate. The indefatigable correspondent of *La Presse* had written to all of the candidates to ask their views and had received just one reply from Senator Poher, which said, "I have many friends in Canada and in Quebec and if you really want to know I make no separation between them." Whatever the new government might do it was clear that Canada and Quebec were low on the agenda and not important to France's interests at the time.

The Embassy opinion was that we were finished with regular public statements about Canada's future. This was just not Pompidou's style. We also believed that the French would continue to support Quebec in its search for an international personality. There were too many Quebec supporters in the government and bureaucracy and they would argue that this subject was a part of Gaullist continuity that could be maintained at little cost to France. This expectation was reinforced by the fact that the French Chamber of Deputies, elected after the Events of May 1968, had a great number of Gaullists amongst its members. It would be in office until 1973. Even so, we expected some gestures to indicate a wish for improved relations with Ottawa. These gestures would be just that and nothing more, for it was inevitable that this dual policy of seeming to have better relations with Ottawa while continuing the traditional Gaullist support for Quebec, thereby maintaining the artificial distinction between Ottawa and Quebec, could only lead to further confrontations with the federal government, particularly in light of the Laurent Affair. We therefore predicted further incidents and a worsening of relations in the short term. There would be ample opportunity for such incidents, with a meeting of Ministers of Education coming later in the year, a projected visit by De Lipkowski in October and the next meeting on La Francophonie early in the following year.

In the longer term, changes to French policy might occur if the number and type of incidents were seen by the French as having an effect on more important relationships, such as that with the United States. Nor would the necessity for these continuing incidents be understood amongst the French public, for while there was general support for assisting the

"Quebec cousins," why did it have to be at the expense of relations with the rest of Canada? With a weaker French government there could be change eventually, perhaps after a series of embarrassments, but we need not expect a serious attempt to reach a *modus vivendi* with Ottawa for some time.[5]

NOTES

1. Ottawa Telegram to Embassy Paris, CA 4, May 31, 1969.
2. Embassy Paris Telegram to Ottawa, no. 1602, June 2, 1969.
3. Embassy Paris Telegram to Ottawa, no. 1630, June 4, 1969.
4. Ottawa Telegram to Embassy Paris, GEU 182, June 16, 1969.
5. Embassy Paris Telegram to Ottawa, no. 1872, June 23, 1969.

12

THE NEW FRENCH GOVERNMENT
THE POLICY OF DUALITY

THE AMBASSADOR GAVE A RECEPTION July 5, 1969 for the International Conference of the Family and for the General Assembly of the International Union of Family Organizations, of which a Canadian had been elected as president. He sent a note to Maurice Schumann inviting him to the reception because of his known interest in social affairs. Schumann came with his wife and was most cordial. It was the first time in many years that a French Foreign Minister had been in the Canadian Ambassador's residence. This action was simply a gesture, but combined with a message for July 1 it indicated a desire to improve the atmosphere of relations between Paris and Ottawa.

Atmosphere was one thing, policy quite another. Five days later President Pompidou gave his first press conference. In answer to a question about relations with Canada, Pompidou said: "We cannot not but have close and friendly relations with the French of Quebec" [he was still using Gaullist phraseology and ignoring the French Canadians outside Quebec] "for historical, racial, linguistic and cultural reasons and these relations are close and excellent. It depends on the government of Ottawa as to whether these relations are prejudicial to good relations between France and Canada."[1] As we had feared, the Paris-Ottawa-Quebec axis was to be part of Gaullist continuity. We therefore faced a government desirous of improving relations with Canada but with no change in the policy of assisting the Quebec government in whatever it requested of France. Since this policy of duality meant continued interference in domestic Canadian affairs, it would be only a matter of time before the next confrontation with the French would occur.

Schumann saw the Ambassador officially for the first time on July 21. Beaulieu was under instructions from Mitchell Sharp to make it clear that the Canadian government intended to deal with its relations with France in a spirit of frankness and good will, in order to find solutions to the various matters in dispute between Ottawa and Paris. If France was willing to approach these problems in the same spirit then solutions should prove possible. If Schumann thought that a dialogue at a higher level would be useful such a suggestion would be welcomed in Ottawa. The Ambassador then raised the question of the Canadian delegation to the next Meeting of Francophone Ministers of Education, that was to be held in Paris. Ottawa hoped that there would be no action by the French government to stop participation of a Canadian delegation on the same basis as at Kinshasa; the Prime Minister of Canada and the Premier of Quebec had already agreed on this formula.[2]

Schumann's replies were all too traditional. With regard to the Meeting of Ministers of Education Quebec had a right to attend such conferences. When the Ambassador pointed out that federal government was responsible for international affairs, Schumann said that France would not object to any formula agreed to by Ottawa and Quebec, but expressed some doubt as to whether there was such an agreement. This doubt was probably a result of Claude Morin's recent visit to Paris.

The French Foreign Minister did not bite on the suggestion of a dialogue at a higher level—Trudeau was anathema to the ultra-Gaullists—but did say that he would be pleased to see Mitchell Sharp at the next Assembly of the United Nations. The atmosphere of the meeting was pleasant, as was usually the case when dealing with Schumann, but it was clear that French policy toward Canada remained fundamentally unchanged: in short, a first friendly contact with both sides repeating their previous policies.

In August we had an entertaining diversion, thanks to the irrepressible Philippe Rossillon. One of his assistants told the Embassy that Rossillon was to head a Linguistic Mission to Quebec in September and would like at the same time to make a little visit to Ottawa. In the new political situation, with De Gaulle no longer on the scene, Rossillon clearly was trying to legitimize his position with Ottawa after the disturbance he had caused the previous year. It was unmitigated cheek, but interesting in the sense that he considered his linguistic responsibilities now required a relationship with Ottawa. External Affairs naturally posed many questions about the purpose of the visit and I went to see Jurgensen about the matter. He was fully in the picture, and had already told Rossillon that he could not go without the approval of the Canadian government. He also took the point that to have Rossillon in Canada in the same time frame as De Lipkowski would be adding fuel to the fire. I mentioned that such a visit would have to be cleared with the Prime Minister's Office, in view of Trudeau's statements on Rossillon's last appearance in Canada. I thought that these considerations would be sufficiently daunting and so it turned out. Jurgensen phoned a few days later to say that he had brought friendly pressure to bear and that Rossillon had decided to postpone his trip for a year, though the Linguistic Mission would go to Canada.

René Pleven, a former Prime Minister under the Fourth Republic and now Minister of Justice, was due to attend an International Conference of Jurists in Montreal in early September. It was agreed that he should visit Ottawa; it would be the first visit by a French Minister since De Gaulle's speech in Montreal. Pleven, who was not a Gaullist, had many Canadian contacts and friends and therefore his visit would not cause waves in Canada or in the Gaullist Party. While making a gesture toward the establishment of a more normal relationship with Ottawa, Pleven saw everyone there who counted, from the Prime Minister on down, and heard the same message, to the effect that Canada was willing to let bygones be bygones and would respond willingly to any gesture of comprehension on the part of the French. Pleven for his part said that the new French government intended to deal with Ottawa and would do nothing to contribute to the disunity of Canada.

To conclude the various initial contacts that had to be made on the arrival in power of the new government, I called on Saint-Légier's replacement at the Elysée, who was the officer at the presidency responsible for foreign affairs. Jean-Bernard Raimond had been a member of Couve De Murville's staff and I had known him when we were colleagues on the North Atlantic Policy Advisory Group of NATO Planners. He was a very different character from Saint-Légier, more ebullient, less careful, but more open. He was to become Foreign Minister in the Chirac government of 1986-1988 and afterward my colleague at the Holy See.

Raimond described the foreign policy of the new Pompidou government as being based on the principles of De Gaulle but as entirely pragmatic, dealing with every problem as it arose. On Franco-Canadian relations he said there would be no changes in French policy but there was no desire for sensational disputes. I told him that there was also no change in Canadian policy and therefore there would be occasions when difficulties would arise. Raimond assured me that, if any serious incidents were to occur, he was at the Embassy's disposal to assist in arriving at a satisfactory solution: all very well if the incident could be discussed through diplomatic channels, but if, as seemed likely from past experience, it was a public dispute, then I did not think he could be of much use to us.[3]

The contradiction in French policy between pursuing De Gaulle's aim of supporting whatever Quebec wished for, while making placatory noises about a desire to improve relations with Ottawa, was bound to create the very incidents that Paris said it did not want. On the one hand, France continued to interfere in Canadian domestic affairs, particularly with regard to Quebec's "international personality," while on the other, Paris told Ottawa that it did not wish to adopt a policy that would affect Canadian national unity. In addition, when the French claimed that they must act on Quebec's wishes it was no longer clear who represented Quebec. The Bertrand government was split between the more traditional Union Nationale ministers, who did not believe that in an election year French assistance was a vote-getter, and the more nationalist ministers, supported by influential civil servants, whose agenda was still to use French assistance in order to achieve an "international personality" as a step toward independence.

To further complicate matters the Quebec "cabal" in Paris, centred on De Lipkowski's office, were concerned by De Gaulle's departure and worked harder than ever to press Quebec's case on the new French government. During that autumn of 1969 there were in fact two pressure groups—one in Paris, the other in Quebec—pushing their governments to maintain the status quo in Franco-Quebec relations.

An explosion was inevitable, and it would be all the greater in Ottawa due to disappointment and frayed nerves arising from the FLQ terrorist campaign and, above all, to frustration with the French, who could not or would not see the effect their policy was having on maintaining the "French Fact" in Canada. The famous French logic was, as Trudeau had told Couve De Murville, completely illogical. Continuing interference by France led to hostile reactions in the rest of the country, and was an encouragement to those who wanted to break Canada up, whereas cooperation between Paris, Ottawa and Quebec within the limits of the Canadian constitution and international law, would strengthen French language and culture in Canada. The explosion came in the next month and was, for all these reasons, much greater than the incident that caused it.

NOTES

1. Embassy Paris Telegram to Ottawa, no. 2066, July 11, 1969.
2. Embassy Paris Telegam to Ottawa, no. 2156, July 21, 1969.
3. Embassy Paris Telegram to Ottawa, no. 2719, September 16, 1969.

13

A DISASTROUS AUTUMN

WE HAD KNOWN for some months that De Lipkowski, who was responsible for relations with Quebec, was due to visit the province, where he had never been. It was the view in Ottawa that a French Secretary of State for Foreign Affairs visiting Canada for the first time must also go to Ottawa. Our contacts at the Foreign Office had told us that they thought he would go if invited, and gave us to understand that they had recommended in this sense to the French government. The Ambassador was therefore instructed to call on De Lipkowski personally to issue such an invitation.

De Lipkowski's response to the invitation was to inform the Ambassador that the matter had already been discussed by the French government, which had come to the conclusion that, in the circumstances, such a visit to Ottawa, coming shortly after the Pleven visit was not possible. According to De Lipkowski there were Gaullist susceptibilities that had to be taken into account and it was necessary to proceed gradually to normalize Franco-Canadian relations. He said his visit was to "deepen" his knowledge of Quebec and to reassure the Québécois that their cooperation with France would not be affected by De Gaulle's departure. There would be no new initiatives: the visit was "touristic," not "political"! The visit to Quebec was not so much directed against Ottawa but dictated by internal considerations that a new government could not ignore. We immediately informed Sharp, who was due to meet Schumann for the first time at the General Assembly in New York on the following day, September 24. We recommended a strong reaction against the kind of visit De Lipkowski planned, for if it took place it would revive all the old problems in the relations between the two countries.

The meeting was a difficult one for both Ministers, as neither side intended to change its policy. Schumann was to discover the intricacies of the Canadian dossier and to realize that charm and gestures were of little

The author with his colleagues in front of the Canadian Embassy in Paris, 1970.
Left to right: Jacques Dupuis, Eldon Black, unknown, William Wood, Gaston
Periard, Claude Charland, Fred Bild, Ian Clark, Paul Boudreau.

use when a sovereign country's ability to conduct its foreign relations was
at stake.[1] Sharp put the Canadian case as follows:

> The Canadian government wanted close relations with France; we had a long
> tradition of good relations between us; these relations had been battered recently
> principally because of how France treated its relations with Quebec; the federal
> government was certainly not against these relations, but they should not be
> developed outside the Government of Canada; as in any other country, and in
> accordance with international law, external relations were under the control of
> the central government; therefore close Franco-Quebec relations can be devel-
> oped provided the federal government is consulted and kept informed; other-
> wise, if other countries established contacts with each province Canada would
> not be one country but split into ten; it was in the interest of France that
> Canada follow a policy of bilingualism and that French-speaking Canadians in
> all parts of the country should feel involved in this policy, including when it
> affects foreign relations [i.e. Francophone Meetings of Ministers of Education.]

Sharp concluded with a plea that the French government should take
these factors into account in its dealings with the province of Quebec.

The discussion then turned to the next Meeting of Ministers of Education, to be held in Paris in December, and quickly became difficult and acrimonious, though the arguments were all too familiar. The French said they had understood that Ottawa had accepted the formula used at Kinshasa and had sent an Aide-Mémoire in that sense. Marcel Cadieux, the Undersecretary who was accompanying Sharp, replied that indeed an Aide-Mémoire had been delivered in which it was made clear that the French did not fully accept the Kinshasa formula. Canada had been invited to the Kinshasa Conference as a sovereign country, while on this new occasion France was merely informing Canada that other provinces could attend the meeting in Paris. It had also informed Quebec of the meeting. In other words France had invited not only Quebec but other Canadian provinces to an international conference without any mention of the federal government, which was responsible for foreign affairs. There was then the usual contention from the French that education was a provincial matter internally and therefore externally, while the Canadians replied that the French had no right to interpret the Canadian constitution and by doing so were interfering in domestic affairs. The explanation just furnished by the French was totally unacceptable to Canada, and Ottawa had prepared a reply to the French Aide-Mémoire. At the end of a long, unpleasant and circular discussion Schumann agreed to consider the Canadian reply.

Mitchell Sharp then raised the question of De Lipkowski's forthcoming visit. When Ottawa had learned of this visit it had, in view of his responsibilities, invited him to the National Capital; Sharp had now been informed that the day before De Lipkowski had turned down this invitation. Sharp then suggested to Schumann that, in the interests of promoting good relations, he review this decision: if a French Secretary of State for Foreign Affairs went to Quebec and not to Ottawa, this action would be interpreted in Canada as meaning that the ambitions of Quebec to establish a separate international personality were supported by France. Schumann argued that De Lipkowski was not really a senior minister, that he had been invited by Marcel Masse before Schumann took office, and that he would not be dealing with foreign affairs but education and cultural cooperation which were his specific responsibilities—so much for his "touristic" visit. Schumann also implied that the visit of Pleven to Ottawa should have satisfied the federal government. Sharp closed the discussion by saying that it would be best if De Lipkowski's visit did not provoke another incident, something most likely to occur if he went to Quebec and not to Ottawa.

Sharp's impression of this difficult encounter was that it had had its uses. The new French Foreign Minister had been given the opportunity to listen personally while his Canadian colleague had offered him a number of clear examples of the way in which French policy led to contradictions and difficulties and was not acceptable to the Canadian government.

The next stage in this diplomatic drama occurred three days later on Sunday evening, September 27 when, at the urgent request of the French Ambassador, who had just returned from New York, Prime Minister Trudeau agreed to receive him at his private residence. The Ambassador told the Prime Minister that he was carrying a personal message from Schumann which turned out to be an oral restatement of the French position on the Meeting of Ministers of Education, and many assurances of good intentions and a plea for Canadian understanding. The Ambassador went on to say that Schumann had been dismayed and surprised by his meeting with Sharp, because the French were under the impression that relations were improving, though of course both sides maintained their principles. The Ambassador had seen his new Prime Minister and President Pompidou recently and there was a unanimous desire to ease relations with Ottawa. While the policy of assistance to Quebec would continue, it would not be directed against Ottawa, for the new French government approached relations in a constructive spirit. As far as the forthcoming Meeting of Ministers of Education was concerned the message graciously stated that there was no objection to Ottawa making whatever arrangements it wished to allow provinces with Francophones to attend. The French could not send an invitation to Ottawa because there was no Minister of Education while France did have an agreement with Quebec on education.

The Prime Minister's reply to all this was limited to the Education Ministers' Conference. He told the Ambassador that the Canadian position had been fully explained, the Canadian government had been invited as a fully sovereign state to Kinshasa and had sent a delegation representing all parties. The so-called Kinshasa formula had been negotiated with Quebec and Canada expected that formula to continue to apply, as we did not want to return to the unpleasantness that had followed the Gabon affair. The Ambassador summed up by saying that he understood Canada was prepared to accept the Kinshasa formula if agreement was reached with Quebec and France would not object to a delegation named by Canada on that basis. [2]

Ottawa's assessment of these conversations was that the French wanted to avoid a confrontation with Ottawa but were still prisoners of

De Gaulle's policy toward Quebec. How far they were willing to reconcile the Gaullist past with the desire for better relations remained to be seen. We had been struck at the Embassy by the fact that at no time had the French Ambassador, in his conversation with the Prime Minister, mentioned the impending visit of De Lipkowski to Quebec. To us that meant that the decision not to go to Ottawa had been confirmed by President Pompidou.

We kept away from the Quai for the next few days while the results of the conversations in New York and Ottawa were being digested. Our contacts at the Quebec Delegation claimed that, in discussions between Schumann and Pompidou, a compromise had been examined whereby De Lipkowski, who was to join the French United Nations Delegation, would pay separate visits to Quebec and Ottawa from New York.

I was called in by the Political Director of the Quai, De Beaumarchais, on October 6, three days before De Lipkowski was due to arrive in Quebec, and was advised that he was not in a position to tell me anything further at that time about a visit to Ottawa. I told him that the federal government considered this a test case of whether there was a real desire on the part of the French government for better relations with Canada and that, if De Lipkowski went only to Quebec, there would inevitably be a strong and firm reaction from Ottawa with unfortunate consequences for Franco-Canadian relations. De Beaumarchais was clearly uncomfortable and, as if to put matters on a different plane, he said that Schumann would be grateful to learn the results of Mitchell Sharp's meeting in New York with Gromyko, the Soviet Foreign Minister, as he himself was about to depart for an official visit to Moscow. It seemed clear from this meeting that we were heading for a showdown and that, whatever happened, the French could not claim that they had not been warned.

At this juncture we suddenly learned that yet another French minister, Joseph Comiti, who had responsibilities for Youth, would be visiting Quebec in the same time frame as De Lipkowski. We took this at the time as an example of adding insult to injury, though we subsequently learned that it was merely bureaucratic lack of coordination. The Secretary General of the Quai D'Orsay first heard of this other visit by reading his morning newspaper. Quebec of course knew of, and indeed had planned, both these visits, evidently believing that the coming blow-up between Ottawa and Paris would be to its advantage.

It was now clear that the visit would take place. In order to ensure that the Canadian position was formally before the French government and that there was a public position before De Lipkowski arrived in Canada, the Ambassador was instructed by Sharp to leave an Aide-Mémoire with the Political Director of the Quai and a press briefing was given in Ottawa on the same day, October 18, 1969. The Aide-Mémoire set out once again the reasons for the Canadian position and the unacceptability of the French attitude, and placed the blame for whatever might transpire during the visit squarely on the shoulders of the French government which had acted in full knowledge of the situation.

The conclusion of the press briefing sets the tone, and as a result of it and De Lipkowski's arrival the next day the press was in full cry:

It is a matter of regret that M. De Lipkowski has confined his visit to Quebec. This decision is particularly unfortunate because it is likely to give rise to questions in the public mind about the French Government's intentions. The Canadian Government is convinced for its part that close and friendly relations between France and Canada are in their mutual interest and that unnecessary incidents of this kind do not serve that interest.

The Canadian Government welcomed the development of exchanges between France and Quebec and has made arrangements to facilitate them. In making these arrangements, however, the Canadian Government has not in any way abdicated its sovereignty or dispensed with the need to be consulted on matters of foreign relations.

The Canadian Government expects to be shown the normal courtesies. The French Government bears responsibility for any unfavourable impact which this incident may have on the course of Franco-Canadian relations. The Canadian Government has so informed the French Government. It is however prepared to reciprocate any effort to build up a normal and constructive relationship between Canada and France.

In extending an invitation to M. De Lipkowski without consulting the Canadian government, the Quebec Government has regrettably done a disservice to relations between France and Canada and to the cause of Canadian unity.

THE VISIT: OCTOBER 9-16, 1969

Given all that had preceded his arrival in Quebec, one might have thought that De Lipkowski would have had enough sense to exercise some discretion in his public behaviour, but he remained true to himself. His inability to keep his mouth shut and the desire of some of his hosts to make of the visit a major event that would embarrass Ottawa led to a procession through the province with De Lipkowski as the prize exhibit. Much worse, he used a press conference to offer his interpretation of the Canadian constitution. He gave the impression that he had come to Quebec to encourage it in its fight for liberation; he had told a recent Canadian visitor that Quebec would be independent in five to ten years, and he supported the thesis that provinces having jurisdiction internally such as education had jurisdiction externally.

The explosive reaction to this performance was in proportion to the disappointed hopes of an improved relationship with France after the departure of De Gaulle. The subject was discussed in the federal cabinet for the first time in nearly two years; the Quebec government was considerably embarrassed and had difficulty in responding to questions in the Assembly. Trudeau made a number of cutting public statements, and while much of the English-language Canadian press was inclined to pass the incident off as another disagreement on protocol, the press in France, most of which had forgotten about Canada, was sufficiently aroused to give the visit and its aftermath considerable coverage. The French government was embarrassed and De Lipkowski became the butt of the opposition newspapers: *Le Canard Enchaîné*, the famous satirical journal, christened him the "Secretary of State for National Provocation."

The Canadian Cabinet considered the affair before De Lipkowski left the country. The general consensus was that:

The Canadian people doubted that the Government was using enough energy to keep the country united and the weakness in the Government's position was the policy of non-escalation. The people did not understand the real issue because the De Lipkowski affair had been characterized as a simple failure to pay homage to the central authority. The Government's case must be clearly restated showing the implications of the French Government's foreign policy and, while demonstrating support for exchanges on cultural and technical matters for the benefit of all Canadians, indicate that they must be done in an organized and rational manner under the umbrella supervision of the Federal Government.[3]

This decision would be implemented by a policy of playing down the importance of the incident as such in Canada but being tough with the French about the conditions for future VIP visits to Canada.

The Prime Minister then delivered a number of speeches, attacking the behaviour of both the French and the Quebec governments in this whole affair. The most important excerpt from one of these speeches, since it caused a strong reaction in French government circles, was as follows: "While De Lipkowski was not an important minister (Schumann's very words) and the incident was not important in itself, it became so if it indicated a desire on the part of the French Government to make more difficult the survival of Canadian unity. For this reason Canada intends to ask France to negotiate adequate procedures in the future by which French ministers desiring to come to Canada will notify the Federal Government and do so sufficiently far in advance." [4]

At this time, in case adequate arrangements with France could not be negotiated and relations deteriorated further, a group was established in External Affairs to study various possible measures of pressure or retaliation that might be used against France, as well as the risks involved in such actions. Though nothing came of these studies Mitchell Sharp alluded to them when he said at a press conference that the federal government had already worked out steps that might be taken if France refused to acknowledge Canadian sovereignty. That such a group was established reflects the apprehension in Ottawa inspired by the continuing terrorist operations of the Front de Libération du Québec (FLQ), the attack on the Prime Minister at the Saint-Jean Baptiste Parade and the march on McGill University. Attitudes were those characteristic of a siege and some ministers in the government convinced themselves that the French intelligence and security authorities were at least partially responsible for, or were assisting the actions of, the FLQ. No definite proof has ever been produced to confirm these views.

It may be worth adding, given my own intelligence and security background, that during the years I was in Paris, we at the Embassy had no contact with the French security and intelligence services, except for security measures for Canadian buildings after the 1970 October Crisis in Canada. Nor were we aware of any aggressive activity on the part of either the French or the RCMP Security Service, though we assumed that the French tried to intercept our communications. In those days there was no representative of the RCMP Security Service at the Embassy and the only RCMP officer in Paris was the traditional sergeant in the Immigration Bureau, responsible for security checks on immigrants to Canada.

FALL-OUT FROM THE VISIT

On the same day as the Cabinet meeting, instructions were sent by Mitchell Sharp to the Ambassador to see Schumann as soon as possible.

We were informed that the government had decided to adopt "a very firm attitude, to affirm its sovereignty, and to prevent further visits by French ministers or senior civil servants creating incidents in which Franco-Canadian relations would suffer."

The Ambassador was instructed to recall the representations Canada had made before the visit: not only had these been ignored, but Canada had received last-minute notification of the visit of a second French minister. The Canadian government had behaved in a moderate fashion in not annulling or postponing these visits, but it could not accept a repetition of these events; the government had decided to propose that France and Canada determine a procedure, the chief element of which would be that any high level visit would be the subject of consultations and have in advance the agreement of the Canadian government. A diplomatic note setting out these considerations was to be left with Schumann and an additional note was to be left at the Quai, repeating the Canadian legal position with regard to sovereignty and the federal government's responsibility for international affairs. The purpose of this approach was to place the French in a position where they could not allege uncertainty about Canadian constitutional requirements and continue, as they had until now, to interpret the Canadian constitution to suit their own interests.[5]

At this point events permitted the French to take evasive action. Schumann was unavailable, being on an extended tour of the Far East, so he instructed De Lipkowski to receive the Ambassador in his place. Since it would have been ridiculous to call on De Lipkowski to complain about his own activities, we turned the Ambassador's instructions into a diplomatic note addressed to Schumann with a request to see him on his return. Meanwhile, in Ottawa the French Ambassador was called in to be given the oral presentation that the Canadian Ambassador had been unable to give to Schumann.

Schumann would be away for another three weeks, but the French press continued to debate the affair and there was pressure on De Lipkowski to take some provisional action. Le Monde expressed surprise that Franco-Canadian relations had not been resolved. The Gaullist newspapers explained at length the French interpretation of the Canadian constitution. The Herald Tribune reported that President Pompidou had personally stopped the visit to Ottawa; we learned this was a leak from De Lipkowski's office, so he was clearly taking action with the approval of the presidency to save his political position.

I had one of my many skirmishes at the Quai when I delivered our second note on the constitution. The French official concerned took the

line that our demand for prior approval of visits went beyond the existing
procedure whereby the French merely notified us of a visit, usually late
and sometimes not at all. This action called into question the very basis
for the Franco-Quebec Agreements and was extremely serious. The official also claimed that De Lipkowski had been extremely careful to keep
his official remarks within the confines of the agreements with Ottawa
and Quebec, using that old cliché of political life, "his remarks had been
distorted by the press." We in fact were never to see, despite many requests,
the actual transcript of what De Lipkowski had said in Quebec. Finally,
the official commented that they were concerned at anything that might
call into question the status of their agreements with Quebec. This was
interesting in that they were beginning to realize that the agreements with
Ottawa and Quebec would come up for renewal the following year.

We had informed De Lipkowski's office that the Ambassador had
instructions to see Schumann and therefore did not need to see him. De
Lipkowski insisted, and Ottawa allowed the Ambassador to go on the
understanding that he listen and say nothing. He did so on October 21,
1969 and the ineffable Secretary of State treated the Ambassador to a long
and involved explanation of his visit to Quebec and to complaints about
the uncalled for reaction of Prime Minister Trudeau to statements he had
never made. The Ambassador listened and came away from the meeting
with the impression that apart from self-justification by De Lipkowski,
the French government, despite its claims to desire a calming of Franco-
Canadian relations, had no intention of changing its position on ministerial visits.

The next day the Quai's official spokesperson said the Canadian note
was under study and that no decision had been taken as to when or even
whether there would be a response. The following day, after the weekly
meeting of the French Cabinet, the official spokesperson said that De
Lipkowski had made a report on his visit to Quebec and made laudatory
remarks about the state of Franco-Quebec cooperation. In answer to a
question the spokesperson said that the initiative of the Canadian Prime
Minister (our diplomatic note) was unexpected and seemed linked to
internal Canadian problems which were of no concern to France.[6] This
seemed to be a categorical rejection of the Canadian proposal on ministerial visits.

The following day in Ottawa, in answer to questions from the press
outside the House of Commons, Mitchell Sharp outlined the reasons for
the Ambassador's meeting with De Lipkowski and, in repeating Ottawa's

position on responsibility for foreign policy, said that no agreements such as those between France and Quebec could alter that fact. He elaborated on this two days later when "he made clear that the federal government believes the period of unilateral dealings between the Quebec government and France on visits to the Province by French Ministers have come to an end."[7] At this stage we appeared to have regressed to transatlantic disputation in public and an unwillingness by either side to seek to change their basic policies. The next stage would be the meeting with Schumann on November 7.

THE DRAWBACKS TO BEING AN OFFICIAL MESSENGER

For nearly two years, I had been making most of the official complaints about French behaviour in Canada to the French Foreign Ministry. This led to many a slight or unofficial snide remark which, while directed to Canada through myself, caused considerable personal stress. It is nothing new for governments who are in dispute with a foreign government to take it out on that government's official representatives. Two examples during the De Lipkowski affair demonstrate some of the pettiness we were up against.

The first incident was not important in itself and the method employed is probably as old as diplomacy, but it was new to me. I called on the Political Director, who had recently dined at my residence, to enquire when or if we might receive a reply to our two recent diplomatic notes on the De Lipkowski visit. I must admit I did not expect an answer, but the form of his evasions might give us a clue as to what to expect. I posed my question and my interlocutor looked at me but did not reply. After a brief pause I repeated my question; still no reply. I waited now for a good three minutes, each of us staring at the other, and I posed my question for the last time. Still no reply, so after another few minutes I got up, thanked him for the clarity of his reply and left his office. It must be admitted that his ploy was effective for it combined silence with rudeness and at the same time conveyed his message.

Much more disagreeable was the next incident, which also occurred while we were waiting to see Schumann. It involved revenge over the Laurent affair, trouble-making by the Quebec Delegation, and an effort to divert attention from De Lipkowski's performance in Quebec by raising another quite false issue. It also required a lack of professionalism on the part of a Canadian press correspondent for it to happen at all. After the Laurent contretemps we had known that De Lipkowski's office and

the Quebec Delegation were peddling a story to the effect that the
Embassy had interfered and brought pressure to bear in order to affect the
outcome of the presidential election campaign. Neither the French nor
the Canadian press believed the story and nothing was printed at the
time.

After De Lipkowski's visit, the story resurfaced with embellishments.
Unfortunately, at this juncture, a new Canadian correspondent had been
posted to Paris and in making the rounds heard the story for the first
time. He came to the Embassy to say that a spokesperson of the Quai
D'Orsay had declared to him that the reason De Lipkowski had not gone
to Ottawa was because of blackmail from the Canadian Embassy during
the election campaign. According to this source, the person concerned
was myself and I had threatened to open the whole dossier on France-
Quebec-Canada relations to Senator Alain Poher, who was running
against President Pompidou. We told this correspondent the full story of
what had actually happened and suggested he consult his other press colleagues who had been in Paris longer than he. We told Ottawa and we
both agreed to play down this obvious provocation.

We had not counted on the ambitions of our inimitable correspondent who, despite the warnings of his colleagues, saw a headline story as
one of his first achievements on arrival in Paris. He therefore sent the
story naming me as the culprit to the CBC who played it as first item on
the evening news. Once this had happened the other correspondents also
had to report the story. Ottawa naturally denied the whole affair, pointing out that the alleged offence had occurred a few days before the final
election run-off, when it was already clear that Pompidou would win. We
found it difficult to believe that the Quai's official spokesperson had
released such a story, so we cross-questioned our doughty correspondent.
It then transpired that he had not heard the story from the Quai's official
spokesperson but from the head of De Lipkowski's ministerial office, and
that it was this gentleman who had for the first time used my name. We
were now faced with a situation that was much less serious than we had
thought. If it had been the Quai's official spokesperson who had released
the story it would have signalled a deliberate attempt on the part of the
French Foreign Ministry to worsen relations at a tense moment between
the two governments.

The next episode in this saga was a call from our American friends to
say that they had received from Washington a statement on the story by
Trudeau, and could I comment? I could not, because Ottawa had not

thought the matter sufficiently important to inform me. After I had made a rather annoyed request I was told that indeed, the Prime Minister had said in the House of Commons that the story was preposterous, and that Canada was discussing with the French procedures to follow in future visits of French ministers. The matter died there and the French press did not report this story at any time. There was a pleasant epilogue to this affair. A number of my friends amongst the Canadian press group were sufficiently embarrassed by having to use the story once it had appeared on the CBC, that they invited my wife and me to dinner to apologize and explain what had happened from their point of view.

PUTTING BACK THE PIECES

By now relations had reached a new low and we did not expect much from the meeting with Schumann. I thought it might be useful to see what the civil servants could do to pick up the pieces, so I asked Jurgensen to lunch with me at one of Paris's best restaurants, where their specialty was his favourite dish. I was sure that he had recommended that De Lipkowski go to Ottawa and, since his advice had not been followed, he might be relatively frank about what had happened and have some ideas about the future. Jurgensen told me that the Quai, including De Lipkowski, had advised Schumann that in order to put relations with Ottawa on a more normal basis and to avoid another incident, it was essential that De Lipkowski visit both Quebec and Ottawa. The Quai had also asked the Quebec Delegate General if the Quebec government would agree, but the latter said he could not answer one way or the other because his government was divided on relations with France.

Schumann had agreed that De Lipkowski should visit Ottawa and then changed his mind when President Pompidou had decided that, for the time being, there was to be no deviation whatsoever from classic Gaullist foreign policy. This decision had been taken for purely internal reasons related to attacks on Pompidou by the Gaullist party purists. The Quai therefore had had to return to its old habits as far as Canada was concerned. De Lipkowski's visit had confirmed the Quai's worst fears and, according to Jurgensen, Schumann had realized that a mistake had been made, but he doubted that there would be a change in policy as long as Pompidou's ruling remained in force.

I reiterated our policy on visits and Jurgensen said he fully understood, and indeed this was the reason for the Quai's actions and recommendations on the De Lipkowski visit. Then, with a frustration that I had never seen him exhibit in the past, he complained that we were in a ridiculous position in that our relations were, if anything, worse than they had been under De Gaulle, and yet the majority of Canadians, including Québécois, and the French too, wanted an end to these incidents. Because of the impasse on visits he thought there would be further incidents but little likelihood of a change of policy on either side, and all civil servants could do was to counsel moderation and gain time. Coming from one of the main activists for the Quebec cause, this was quite an admission.[8]

The much postponed meeting which would give Schumann the opportunity to respond to our notes took place on November 7. He insisted that he would receive the Ambassador with De Lipkowski in attendance, no doubt to show support for his colleague as a wronged party. I decided to attend with the Ambassador so that he would not be bullied by this twosome, and so Canada could also have a wronged party in attendance. Schumann opened the meeting by referring to his remarks about Canada in answer to questions during the debate on foreign policy which had taken place the previous evening in the National Assembly. He said these remarks should be read as expressing a desire not to further envenom relations between the two countries. We had not seen them since they had not been reported in the press, but in effect he had merely said that not all visits by French ministers to Quebec automatically required a visit to Ottawa. Since Ottawa had never made such a requirement, this was not very earth-shattering, but as he had claimed it did not make matters worse.

The Ambassador then followed the instructions he had received from Sharp on the Canadian proposal regarding future visits by French ministers. Schumann responded that French visits to Quebec were sanctioned by the Franco-Canadian Cultural Agreement and did not require consultation with or agreement by the federal government. When the Ambassador suggested that the French government might wish to review this policy Schumann went off on a tangent, saying he could have made relations between the two countries much worse during the foreign policy debate by referring to the personal attacks made on De Lipkowski (by Trudeau). He was much pained by these attacks, which were completely unjustified. De Lipkowski smiled. The Ambassador repeated the Canadian position, including the need for notification of visits sufficiently far in advance so that Canada could either agree or not agree to a visit taking place. Schumann wanted to know whether the Canadian government reserved the right to refuse or to agree to future visits, which would be a new element in our relations. The Ambassador did not reply and both sides rested on their positions.[9]

My own impressions of this confrontation were contained in a letter I wrote the same day to John Halstead, Head of the European Division. The French had now been advised at the senior ministerial level, that Canada intended to be firm on its visits policy. I had detected a definite wish for a calming of the rhetoric on both sides of the Atlantic. I did not think we would receive a reply to our notes, nor did I think there would be a French ministerial visit to Canada for some time. Any visits by Canadian ministers to Paris should be handled carefully with plenty of advance notice, so that the French could not accuse us of the same sins that they had committed. A more normal relationship would have to await events such as the forthcoming Meeting of the Francophone Ministers of Education and the next rendezvous of Sharp and Schumann during the regular Ministerial Meeting of NATO in Brussels.[10]

These two events occurred at much the same time in early December 1969 and both contributed to the process of "picking up the pieces." When the Ministers met they were both conscious of the extent to which relations had deteriorated since their last meeting and of the need to reverse the trend, at least insofar as the atmosphere surrounding Franco-Canadian relations was concerned. Sharp picked up a remark from Schumann about the need for calm and said Canada was of the same view, and that possibly the best way would be to agree on a number of discreet but positive steps, such as, for example, a visit in the New Year by an appropriate French minister whose responsibilities would not complicate relations with the provinces. Schumann agreed, but said he could not agree that every French minister visiting Quebec had to visit Ottawa, though every invitation from Canada would be sympathetically considered. Sharp riposted that Canada had never taken the position that every French minister had to come to Ottawa, though in the circumstances surrounding De Lipkowski's visit it would have been advisable for him go to Ottawa, as Sharp had warned Schumann at their last meeting. Schumann did not entirely agree, as some statements about the visit—such as those of Trudeau—were not helpful. Sharp said "we had been provoked," but that if France wished to make a new start we could explore the possibility of future visits that would not lead such incidents. Schumann agreed.

At this point Sharp told Schumann that he had been invited to open the new wing of the Maison Canadienne at the University of Paris and, while he did not know if he could attend, he would like to know if such a visit would be welcomed by the French. Schumann replied was in effect: "You are the Foreign Minister of a friendly and allied country and if you come I will invite you to lunch."

The rest of the meeting was essentially a restatement by both sides of their positions on visits and while Schumann did not make any concessions, his tone was neither argumentative nor aggressive, so Sharp decided not to push him further at the time. [11] At a press conference after the meeting Sharp said that both Ministers had talked about the De Lipkowski incident, had agreed that there was room for improvement in Franco-Canadian relations and now considered the incident to be past history. When asked if there was now a new era and a return to normal relations with France Sharp replied that, while both Ministers would like to see relations restored to normal and avoid incidents and this was encouraging, "there was no change in the fundamental positions of both sides." [12] The Canadian assessment of the meeting was that we had gained—and this was no mean achievement—a period of truce. Since there were forthcoming events, such as the Second Niamey Conference on La Francophonie, that could destroy this truce, we must use the interim period to build on the Ministers' meeting.

Prime Minister Trudeau and Premier Bertrand had negotiated an ad hoc agreement on the Canadian Delegation to the Education Ministers' Meeting in Paris. It was based on the precedent of Kinshasa, but this time the Canadian Delegation would be led by the Quebec Minister of Education, and would include the other interested provinces and counsellors from the federal government. The Quebec Education Minister was now Jean-Marie Morin who, while not a powerful minister, was an honest and practical man resolved, unlike certain of his colleagues, to abide by the agreement entered into by his Premier. He met with the Canadian delegation before the conference and took them through the terms of the agreement so that there could be no misunderstanding. Some of the Quebec civil servants were clearly unhappy, but there were no incidents and the Delegation was able to concentrate on the substance of the conference. Two positive developments from this meeting were: the precedent established, and followed thereafter, whereby the Quebec Minister of Education of the day led Canadian delegations to this set of conferences; and the French acceptance for the first time, at these Conferences, of the fact that there was a Canadian delegation led by a provincial minister.

In a personal letter to John Halstead of December 12, I attempted to draw conclusions about these recent events and to suggest priorities for the first half of 1970. I thought that the current circumstances called for a further attempt to regulate our relations with France, as there were some signs of a new attitude in Paris. Laurent, now the Secretary General of Education, had gone out of his way to tell me that he had been pleased by the positive nature of the Sharp-Schumann meeting; the Secretary General of the Presidency, who was planning Pompidou's forthcoming visit to Washington, had told my American opposite number that there would be no more De Lipkowski-type incidents; and De Lipkowski had told a member of the Canadian delegation to the Education Conference that his Canadian trip had finished his political career, and his friends had told him he was in the wrong. This statement was typical hyperbole, but he had felt the need to pass the message on. We knew, however, from the problems that were arising about the forthcoming Second Niamey Conference, that the ultra-Gaullists throughout the administration and the National Assembly still had considerable influence.

What was needed was a continuing dialogue at a high level on a regular basis. Unfortunately we did not have an Ambassador who could engage in such a dialogue in Paris at that time. The alternative was to hold regular ministerial meetings, and I suggested that a minister be sent to the 20th Anniversary of the France-Canada Association whose new President, Senator Garet, was a friend of Schumann and wanted to highlight the occasion. I also counselled against Sharp coming to the Maison Canadienne. The Quebec government provided a major subsidy, a Quebec minister would be in attendance and the event was in the field of education. I thought Quebec should be the major star on this occasion. Much more appropriate would be a visit by Sharp in April 1971 to open the Cultural Centre, a project of the federal government. This advice was taken. Meanwhile we should be following up Sharp's suggestion of a visit to Ottawa by a French minister with responsibilities in a non-controversial field. Regarding this matter I had already seen Jurgensen, who was encouraging, and Raimond at the Elysée, who was not discouraging.

My view of where Franco-Canadian relations stood at the end of a topsy-turvy period was that the year's events had left Canada in a stronger position to confront the dual French policy toward Ottawa and Quebec. It had also left a legacy of suspicion and rancour on all sides that only time and a constructive dialogue would efface. We had to convince doubters on both sides of the Atlantic that it was possible for Paris and Ottawa to cooperate on substantive matters and that it was not true, as had often been claimed, that cooperation could only take place between Paris and

Quebec. The challenge was to find areas of substantive cooperation that were clearly to the advantage of both countries.

NOTES

1. Can. Del. New York Telegram to Ottawa, no. 2166, September 24, 1969.
2. Ottawa Telegram to Embassy Paris, no. 51185, October 2, 1969.
3. Cabinet Minutes, nos. 62-69, October 15, 1969.
4. *Montreal Gazette*, October 23, 1969.
5. External Affairs Telegram to Embassy Paris, G 277, October 15, 1969.
6. Embassy Paris Telegram to Ottawa, no. 3158, October 22, 1969.
7. Ottawa Telegram to Embassy Paris, W 134, October 22, 1969.
8. Embassy Paris Telegram to Ottawa, no. 3317, November 3, 1969.
9. Embassy Paris Telegram to Ottawa, no. 3390, November 7, 1969.
10. Personal Letter, Black-Halstead, November 7, 1969.
11. Can. Del. NATO Telegram to Ottawa, no. 3331, December 5, 1969.
12. Can. Del. NATO Telegram to Ottawa, no. 3324, December 5, 1969.

14

MUCH ADO ABOUT VISITS

ONLY TOO OFTEN in those years, after it had been agreed that a dispute should be put behind us, unforeseen events would arise to further complicate Franco-Canadian relations. The meeting in December between Schumann and Sharp, with its aim to try by reciprocal ministerial visits to improve relations, was followed in January by Prime Minister Trudeau's unexpected skiing holiday in France and the sudden arrival of Marcel Masse to visit De Lipkowski in his Royan constituency and call on French ministers in Paris.

This was the second time within a few months that the Prime Minister had passed through Paris. In the late summer he had been on his way to a yacht moored at Cannes. Now he was on his way to ski at Courchevel in the French Alps. We were suddenly informed that he was coming, that the Canadian press knew he was going through Paris, and that the Prime Minister did not wish to meet the press on French soil: would we please take evasive action! When he arrived we took him to a private suite in the airport and dressed one of our officers to resemble the Prime Minister from a distance; this individual, surrounded by a group of Embassy personnel, dashed down to the Ambassador's limousine and headed into the city. The press bit and followed, only to discover, when the car arrived at the Embassy an hour later, that the Prime Minister was not in it. Before they could return to the airport Trudeau was on his way to Courchevel. It took some time for us to re-establish our previous relationship with the Canadian press correspondents.

The arrival in France of a Prime Minister who was certainly unconventional by French standards was fully covered by the Paris press, and a number of journalists were dispatched to Courchevel to expatiate on his skiing prowess and try for an interview. He refused to see the press but an enterprising lady journalist cornered him at the top of a ski lift! We opened the conservative, and in those days staid, *Le Figaro* the next morning to see a cartoon figure on the front page, clearly our Prime Minister, skiing down a hill and shouting "Vive le Schuss libre." On the back page was a three-page column in which he answered a few questions. "Why was he skiing in Courchevel when there were so many other places he could have chosen?" "I miss France, I had hoped to come last year but it was not possible. The General was still there." "How did he view the future of Franco-Canadian relations?" "I met Pompidou a long time ago and we spoke at length but right now I don't know what we could say to each other." "I would have liked to stay in Paris on my return to Canada but there are diplomatic difficulties, Mr. De Lipkowski did not stop at Ottawa."[1] Needless to say these remarks were not appreciated by the Gaullists or the Elysée and made a meeting between Pompidou and Trudeau highly unlikely. Indeed the closest Trudeau would ever come to Pompidou was at the latter's funeral some three years later.

The Prime Minister did have a stopover of a few hours at Orly airport on his return and he and I discussed the state of play between Ottawa and Paris. Our conversation revolved around the question of what to do about the Cultural Agreements between France and Canada and France and Quebec, which were due for renegotiation in 1970. The Prime Minister said that, since France had linked the question of official visits to Canada and these Agreements during the De Lipkowski affair and, since any future French high level visits to Canada would have to have the approval of the federal government, it would seem best to enter into a negotiation with the French this year and insist on a clause to regulate French activities in Canada. I replied that I was sure the French would refuse such a clause and accuse the federal government of calling into question both Agreements in an attempt to stop cooperation between France and Quebec. This did not seem to worry the Prime Minister, though he agreed that an unwritten understanding, during the negotiations, on the handling of future visits might be acceptable.

I observed that if we let the occasion of renegotiation go by this year we would continue to be faced with France's dual policy toward Ottawa and Quebec, but if we renegotiated in the manner suggested by the Prime Minister, we risked bringing down the whole fabric of cooperation between France and Canada and France and Quebec. The question to be answered in Ottawa was whether we were able and willing, by forcing a renegotiation, to run the risk of a major confrontation with both France and Quebec. The Prime Minister's only comment on this was that, given the policy of the French government, there did not seem to be much point in going out of our way to seek to cooperate. Civil servants do not expect policy decisions from prime ministerial stopovers at airports but at least he had focused on what would be a major decision on our relations with France in the coming year.[2]

During this same stopover the Prime Minister informed the Beaulieus that, in view of the Ambassador's state of health, he would be replaced during the coming summer. This message was later confirmed by External Affairs and, since the visits of Gérard Pelletier and Mitchell Sharp were likely to take place before that time, the Ambassador was instructed to take sick leave for three months outside France. I would be formally in charge during these ministerial visits.

On the same day that the Prime Minister left France the incorrigible Marcel Masse, now Minister of Intergovernmental Affairs, arrived, having received an invitation from the equally incorrigible De Lipkowski to visit him in his constituency at Royan. Masse was in Europe with no particular program but seemed to be conducting a pre-electoral campaign which included a number of anti-federalist speeches. Presumably he thought his actions in Europe would impress his constituents. If so, he was to be proved sadly mistaken.

While in Royan, Masse attended a rally organized by De Lipkowski before an invited audience and the press, at which the French Minister delivered a rambling speech in an obvious attempt to explain his actions in Quebec and put the blame on Ottawa for the subsequent publicity. There was a Canadian press correspondent at this affair, and the first news we heard of it came from an article in the *Ottawa Citizen* entitled "France claims Intimidation."[3] According to the article De Lipkowski had claimed that if the General had been in power his visit would have been routine, but since he had gone the federal government had wanted to feel the pulse of the Pompidou regime to see if it would abandon its program of cooperation with Quebec. There had been no problems when Pearson was in power—the speaker passed airily over the General's visit to Quebec and his support for Quebec independence—but the present federal government seemed to have realized that Franco-Quebec cooperation was reinforcing Quebec's wish to be French and Ottawa could not wring the neck of Quebec's aspirations so easily ... and so on. Masse was reported to have said at the same meeting that he was not optimistic that Quebec would be able to attain its goals within Confederation.

We were able to obtain a transcript of De Lipkowski's speech, so we knew that the *Citizen* had correctly reported his remarks. We brought the article to the attention of the Quai, who were embarrassed but could not believe that De Lipkowski had been correctly reported, since his remarks were contrary to the agreement reached at the last meeting between Schumann and Sharp.

Meanwhile, Masse had moved on to Paris, where he met French ministers and was given lunch by Schumann. He was the first Quebec minister to come to Paris to discuss Quebec's relations with France since De Gaulle had left power some eight months before, an indication of the level of priority given those relations by the Bertrand government. Nothing significant transpired from the visit: Masse concentrated on the lack of French investment in Quebec and the French complained about the difficulties encountered by French exports to Quebec. Masse delivered a nationalist speech to the Diplomatic Press Club in Paris, but when it was not reported in the French press he cancelled his planned press conference and departed for London. Masse was back in France a few days later to go skiing at Courchevel. Imitation is not always a form of flattery.

Ottawa was, with reason, annoyed by these events and wanted to protest to the French and confront them with the transcript of De Lipkowski's speech. At the Embassy we argued that, having already brought De Lipkowski's remarks to the attention of the Quai, we should ignore the parish pump politics of Masse and De Lipkowski and concentrate our efforts on the future visits of Mitchell Sharp to Paris and a French minister to Ottawa. At this point the French Ambassador in Ottawa, on instructions, informed the federal government that his government assumed, as had been agreed by the two Foreign Ministers, that Sharp would be visiting Paris to open the Canadian Cultural Centre and that the only matter to be resolved was the timing. The Ambassador also raised the question of a visit by a French minister whose responsibilities were in a domain of federal competence and suggested the Secretary of State for Defence, André Fanton.[4]

This move was a cunning one on the part of the French, for by sending a Gaullist minister of the same rank as De Lipkowski—he was an assistant to Debré, the high priest of Gaullism—they could tell the ultra-Gaullists that Sharp's visit was unofficial; Fanton worked in a domain where Quebec had no jurisdiction and did not claim any. Their game plan was to link these two visits and, once they were out of the way, to return to the original policy of sending French ministers to Quebec when necessary, thus ignoring Ottawa's note requiring consultation before any such visit. We argued with Ottawa that, by accepting this French suggestion,

Canada was falling into a trap. Canada would have two courtesy visits without any progress being made on practical cooperation, progress which could occur if the government adhered to its original plan to invite a "technical" minister in the scientific area. Ottawa thought we were too pessimistic (if we were, it was not surprising after the last few years), that they had an ace in the hole because of the requirement to renew the Franco-Canadian Cultural Accord, an election was forthcoming in Quebec, and Sharp intended to have substantive discussions on relations when he came to Paris.

Support for Ottawa's opinion came in a long analysis of Pompidou's foreign policy by André Fontaine, editor of *Le Monde*, who had recently dined with the President and Maurice Schumann. In Canada "a process of normalization was being followed which could lead to a visit to Paris by the Minister of Foreign Affairs, Sharp, with whom Maurice Schumann had already had cordial meetings; this policy should in no way suggest to the Québécois that France does not support their objective": still the policy of duality but with more balance than in the past. Before these visits could take place, however, there was a large hurdle to be overcome, namely French support for Quebec's international personality at the forthcoming Conference in Niamey to establish La Francophonie.

NOTES

1. *Le Figaro*, January 8, 1970.
2. Personal Letter, Black-Halstead, January 16, 1970.
3. External Affairs Telegram to Embassy Paris, GEU 192, February 23, 1970.
4. External Affairs Telegram to Embassy Paris, PDF 54, January 13, 1970.

15

THE SECOND NIAMEY CONFERENCE
HOSTILITIES IN AFRICA: ROUND THREE

IN THE YEAR following the decision of the first Niamey Conference to establish a small multilateral development organization (the Agence Francophone) the acting Secretary, Jean-Marc Léger, together with President Diori of Niger in his capacity as convenor of the Conference, worked out a provisional Charter for the Agence. Léger had visited all possible participants to obtain their reactions and Diori made a state visit to Canada. As Léger proceeded the French became increasingly dissatisfied with him; in their eyes he was trying to create a sizeable multilateral aid agency rather than a small office essentially controlled from France. Léger was also, according to the French, taking on the airs of an independent international Secretary General: he discussed experience with the Secretary General of the Commonwealth, a fellow Canadian, and was not a good administrator. The French view of the Agence had not changed. They did not want it, because it might interfere with their own bilateral development relationships, and if they had to have it, it should be as small as possible, with their own nominee as Secretary General. Léger had been a disappointment to them, a curious anomaly: an independently minded Canadian who was also a Quebec *indépendantiste*.

At the Embassy we had not been involved in these developments, occurring as they did in Africa or Canada; Ottawa had a foreign service officer working in Léger's group. This situation changed suddenly on January 21, 1970 when I found waiting for me at my office an unannounced messenger from President Diori. The gentleman, who was French, presented himself as Special Counsellor to President Diori, with a message for the Canadian and French governments with regard to the Conference. We later discovered that he was not a Special Counsellor but rather a French government counsellor to Diori and therefore a member of Foccart's intelligence network in the former French colonies.

This man told me that President Diori had need of a reply within 48 hours from our Prime Minister as to whether or not Canada approved of the draft constitution for the Conference and whether there would be a Canadian delegation including Quebec. The reason for urgency was that Diori was due to meet in three days time with his fellow African heads of state at Yaoundé and was required to present a progress report on the Conference. If he did not receive a reply he intended to tell his colleagues that internal problems in some countries—meaning Canada—with regard to the constitution meant that the Conference could not be held in March as planned. Diori thought that it would then have to be postponed indefinitely and that the Agence would not be established. He intended in any case to resign his responsibility for hosting the Conference. By pushing Ottawa to the wall Diori would either receive assurances that he could go ahead without risk of the antics that had marred the first Niamey Conference, or if an inadequate answer was received and he had to postpone, neither the French nor his African colleagues could blame him for the collapse of the Conference.

By this time the first negotiations between Ottawa and Quebec on the Conference had taken place, and it quickly became apparent that there were considerable differences between the two sides. Ottawa was generally satisfied with the draft constitution of the Agence, since it was based on the sovereignty of states and only countries could sign the convention establishing the Agence and become members. Not surprisingly, Quebec disagreed with the draft constitution and tabled an Aide-Mémoire prepared by Claude Morin. This document put forward amendments to the draft constitution that ensured Quebec would become a member of the Agence with full rights, separately from Canada, and that these rights could be extended to those other provinces that had attended the founding Conference in Niamey, namely Ontario and New Brunswick. In addition, Quebec wanted to chair the Canadian delegation, to have the Canadian member on the Board of the Agence named by Quebec, and to have any formal decisions by the Agence signed by the provinces as well as Canada. After asking for the moon, Quebec greatly weakened its negotiating position by stating that it would only pay five percent of the Canadian share of the budget of the Agence. Once again Quebec demonstrated that its main aim was to establish an international role, not to contribute to development aid in Francophone Africa.[1]

Ottawa rejected these demands because they accorded Quebec an international personality distinct from that of Canada within the Agence, which was to be created by an international convention signed by sovereign states. It offered as a counterproposal that Quebec would be given a special role within the Agence as long as such a role did not permit Quebec to acquire an international personality distinct from that of Canada. So negotiations were engaged and Ottawa was confident of an agreement, since the Bertrand government would face an election shortly and was not interested in creating another international incident with Ottawa. What Ottawa did not know was that Claude Morin's position paper was already in the hands of the French and had probably been one of the subjects discussed by Marcel Masse during his recent visit to Paris.

Ottawa's reaction to the message from Niger was swift and comprehensive. Prime Minister Trudeau replied in general terms—it was assumed the French, given the messenger, would read the letter—that Canada was satisfied with the draft constitution of the Agence, it could be distributed to other interested countries and Canada would attend the Conference with suitable representation from the provinces. At the same time our man in Africa, Michel de Goumois, was instructed to see Diori and elaborate on the Prime Minister's letter as follows: Canada was not in any way hindering progress toward establishing the Agence and could not accept responsibility for any delay. Ottawa was willing to tell Diori, as a friend of Canada, that the normal process of consultation with interested provinces, including Quebec, was now engaged, and in the light of precedent the process would be lengthy but have positive results. Ottawa expected the Canadian delegation to Niamey to be broadly representative and to play a constructive role. It also expected that the invitation to participate in the Conference would be sent to the Canadian government, which would be responsible for organizing the delegation to go to Niamey.

When de Goumois saw President Diori he found him quite willing to accept the Trudeau message as elaborated and he promised to make no mention of Canada in speaking to his African colleagues about his difficulties with the Conference. He was now much more concerned about the pressure exerted on him by the French. He had received an Aide-Mémoire from the French on their conditions for attending the Conference. This document mentioned the Canadian situation and outlined Quebec's views in the same terms as the paper prepared by Claude Morin for negotiations with the federal government. The French also stated that, since there was no agreement between Ottawa and Quebec at that time, both should be represented at the Niamey Conference. This latest example of French interference in Canadian affairs had led Diori to question once again whether he should go ahead with the Conference. Finally, after another round of African consultations, he decided to proceed and announced the dates for the Conference to his fellow African heads of state at Yaoundé. [2]

The next problem to arise was familiar: who would receive an official invitation to the Conference? Diori decided, as was appropriate, to send an invitation to the Canadian government only and not one to Quebec. He covered himself by obtaining the agreement of the other African heads of state and in order to hold off the French he told us of another tactic he wished to use. He intended, with Ottawa's approval and as a matter of courtesy, to send a letter of thanks to the four premiers—of Quebec, Ontario, Manitoba and New Brunswick—who had received him during his Canadian trip and at the same time inform them of the date of the Conference. These letters were not to be official and were not invitations. This put Ottawa in a difficult position, as it had to ensure that Diori's proposed letters did not compromise Canada's international position or alter its relationships with the provinces. To avoid these dangers, we asked, and Diori agreed, that the letters should be drafted jointly.

While this process was underway the French intensified the pressure on Niger by sending a messenger with a letter signed by De Lipkowski in the name of the President of the Republic and Maurice Schumann, demanding that Quebec receive a separate invitation. It became clear that similar messages had been sent to the other African heads of state. Diori was not too concerned about this new French pressure, but he was shocked by its effect on some of the other heads of state who kept calling on him to send an invitation to Quebec. He told De Goumois that the French behaviour made him realize how insignificant was the independence of his own country in such a battle. This was one of the reasons why he attached such importance to his links with Canada, as they provided him with a counterweight to France and could help to ensure that the word "independence" for his country was not entirely empty of meaning. The letters to the premiers went off, but the French campaign for a separate Quebec invitation continued, accompanied by a campaign of disinformation alleging Canadian lack of interest in La Francophonie.

We argued, from the Embassy perspective, that it was now time once again to make clear to the French what Canadian policy on the creation of La Francophonie was, and our attitude toward separate invitations to provinces. Those leading the fight in Paris for a separate Quebec's international personality—De Lipkowski, Jurgensen and others—were able to do so because of their offices, but their weakness was that they could not afford another public Franco-Canadian scandal. We also argued that Canada should not disassociate its Francophonie policy from normalizing our bilateral relations with France, but rather make it clear to the French that they were linked. France could not continue its behaviour with regard to the Niamey Conference and expect better relations with Canada from the forthcoming Sharp and Fanton visits. The reason why the French were interfering so blatantly on this occasion was that they and their Quebec friends realized that, if Niamey were successful, there would be a juridical foundation for international francophone relations which would prove difficult to change. The Quebec activists knew that this was the last opportunity for some time to insert a foot in the international door. Their French supporters believed that a separate role for Quebec was essential to their own policy of duality toward Canada, a policy that "normalized" relations with Ottawa through some ministerial visits, while maintaining privileged extra-constitutional links with Quebec.[3]

Ottawa decided to counterattack. Our ambassadors in Francophone Africa were instructed to see the heads of state to whom they were accredited to explain, once again, the reasons for Canadian support for the Agence and La Francophonie, and why Ottawa could not accept a separate Quebec international personality. The French Ambassador in Ottawa, who was about to leave for Paris, was called in on the instructions of the Prime Minister, to carry a message to President Pompidou along the following lines: France had recently expressed a desire to normalize relations with the federal government and had expressed an intention to not intrude into Canadian internal affairs. Ottawa was astonished to learn that French diplomatic representatives in Africa were exercising pressure on African states to ensure a separate Quebec invitation to the Niamey Conference. This hardly coincided with a desire to normalize relations and was certainly a further intervention in Canada's internal constitutional affairs. Such action could not only negatively affect Franco-Canadian relations, but also put at risk the establishment of the Agence Francophone, an objective of Canadian foreign policy and, we believed, of French policy as well. It had been agreed at the previous Niamey Conference that the Agence would be a multilateral organization, created by sovereign states acting on the principle of respect for the sovereignty of each member state. Canada held strongly to these principles and could not accept that a province could aspire to be a fully independent member of the Agence, as this would inevitably oppose it to the rest of the country; Canada would therefore oppose any initiative that would create such a situation.[4]

I was instructed to see my contact at the Elysée to make the same points and to ensure that President Pompidou was aware, both through his Ambassador in Ottawa and myself at the Embassy in Paris, of the position of the Canadian government. I saw Raimond at the Elysée on March 6 and carried out my instructions. I also reminded him of our arrangement, whereby I would only come to see him if serious difficulties appeared likely to arise between our two governments. Raimond's only comment was to the effect that if Ottawa and Quebec came to an agreement on Niamey and the Agence, he did not foresee any problems at the Conference. He also assured me that Trudeau's message and my *démarche* were fully understood at the Elysée. I reported to Ottawa that, despite what might seem to be a conciliatory reaction on Raimond's part, the Embassy believed that there would be no change in French tactics supporting Quebec, and that a confrontation at Niamey seemed inevitable.[5]

This quickly proved to be the case. A few days later we learned of the French position for the Niamey Conference as it had been delivered to President Diori. The French clearly had not changed their objective of obtaining Quebec's entry into the Agence. They were now proposing that a whole group of Francophone institutions be part of the organization, including universities, societies such as certain Acadian groups and the province of Quebec. Since there was no comparison between these associations and a government, such as that of Quebec, this was obviously an opening bargaining position. The French position also limited the scope of the Agence through a series of regulations and a small budget, so it could not affect France's bilateral development relations in Africa.

Meanwhile, through Foccart's African network, a campaign was underway against President Diori, suggesting that he should not preside over the Conference he was convening because he was anti-French. On the other hand, various French sources were telling Diori and ourselves that this was all the work of De Lipkowski and his cohorts, and that while President Pompidou wanted to do something for Quebec, he did not want to upset the African heads of state. This was the classic diplomatic ploy whereby you allow some of those under your orders to create maximum havoc in order to achieve your objective, while at the same time outwardly observing the proprieties, thus leaving open an avenue of escape in case the scheme backfires.

While these disturbances arose in anticipation of the Niamey Conference, Quebec and Ottawa had come to an agreement on the composition and methods of operation of the Canadian delegation. They were much the same as for the first Niamey Conference; Gérard Pelletier, the Secretary of State, would lead the delegation and the Deputy Chief of the Delegation was to be Julien Chouinard, a senior Quebec civil servant and trusted adviser to Premier Bertrand. There were to be no Quebec ministers because of the forthcoming election, and no Claude Morin (though he was in Niamey in spirit) thanks to his original Aide-Mémoire. Chouinard was known as a man who kept his word and would not renege on his instructions as Marcel Masse had done at the previous Niamey Conference.

This then was the atmosphere in which Gérard Pelletier and his delegation arrived in Paris, where he was to attend the celebrations of the Twentieth Anniversary of the France-Canada Association, before proceeding on to Niamey. The Embassy had considered the Association somewhat folkloric, more interested in trips to Canada by its members than in Canada itself. We therefore had concentrated our efforts on the Franco-Canadian Institute, which was more business-oriented and provided a more convincing platform for visiting Canadian ministers. The new President of the Association, Senator Garet, hoped to inject life into it by widening its focus so as to appeal younger French men and women, who might be attracted to a dynamic North American society which was partially French-speaking and not in the U.S.

This Annual Congress of the Association proved to be a successful launch pad for Senator Garet's ideas—instead of the usual attendance of two hundred over five hundred members were present. At the traditional Embassy reception, four hundred guests were expected and seven hundred turned up, many of them telling us that this was the first occasion they had had since De Gaulle had left power to express their affection for Canada as a whole. The meetings took place in the Senate, where Gérard Pelletier delivered a major speech on the bilingual and bicultural nature of the policies of the federal government and the Canadian expectation that France would contribute to these policies. Events finished with mass in the superb thirteenth century Sainte-Chapelle; Maurice Schumann attended, presumably in his "normalization of relations" mode. It should be added that Senator Garet had deliberately excluded De Lipkowski from participating.

Pelletier had asked to see Maurice Schumann before leaving for Niamey, to try to discover whether there were, in the view of the French

Foreign Minister, any nuances in the French position as presented to Diori. Schumann proved elusive but the egregious De Lipkowski proposed to receive Pelletier, who politely refused. Then, at the last minute, Schumann said he could see Pelletier after the mass, and arrangements were made to meet in the office of Senator Poher, President of the Senate and the defeated candidate in the presidential election. There were a number of ironies in this meeting. Here was a Canadian Minister seeing a French Foreign Minister, who was about to tell him of France's latest interference in Canadian affairs, in the office of a politician defeated by his own President, and the Minister was accompanied by a Canadian civil servant alleged to have interfered in that same presidential election. Why Schumann changed his mind and saw Pelletier remains a mystery, but I assumed he wanted the head of the Canadian delegation to hear that the position he would be confronted with in Niamey was supported at a high level in Paris.

Pelletier opened the meeting by asking for an explanation of the French position on participation in the Agence. Schumann developed the thesis that, to give the Agence greater flexibility, a place should be found for other Francophone groups such as cultural societies, university associations and the province of Quebec. If this line were followed the Quebec problem would be avoided, since there would be organizations other than Quebec attached to the Agence. Pelletier then asked whether the French envisaged consultative status for these organizations, or whether they were to have the same status as sovereign states. There was no clear answer, but it became evident that the French, by following this convoluted course, hoped to enable Quebec to play its own separate role in the Agence. The Secretary of State finally asked how the French could reconcile the status of international or national Francophone societies with a political entity such as the province of Quebec. Again no reply—hardly surprising, since there was no way of reconciling the irreconcilable. While we had not expected Schumann to change the French position, and he was obviously uncomfortable with its logic, it was clear that the Pompidou government was holding firm to its dual policy regarding Canada.

The meeting concluded with Pelletier informing Schumann that he had spoken a few hours earlier with Trudeau, who had asked him to ensure that Schumann understood that Canada considered it fundamental that the Agence be created and controlled by the sovereign states that were participating in it, but would agree to some form of consultative status for the sort of Francophone organization mentioned in the French position paper. I told Ottawa when reporting on this meeting that I remained convinced that the French would continue to insist on a separate role for Quebec, in expectation of creating conflict within the Canadian delegation and the conference, and of furthering their additional aims of either torpedoing the Agence or at least diluting its capacity to have a meaningful role in African development aid.

When Pelletier and his delegation arrived at Niamey he was met with a message that President Diori wished to see him urgently. He found the President depressed by continuous pressure from the French, who disliked his concept of La Francophonie—with which the other African states agreed—and his policy toward Canada. He was greatly relieved to hear from Chouinard, who had accompanied Pelletier, that instructions from Premier Bertrand were to the effect that he wanted no incidents during the Conference, which was taking place during the Quebec election campaign.

The French attack on the draft constitution of the Agence and Canada's position within it started the same day, when the two ministers in charge of the French delegation, and their senior adviser, none other than our old nemesis Jurgensen, called on Pelletier. They presented a revised constitution for the Agence, designed to ensure separate Quebec membership. One stipulation was to the effect that any government which had competence in a particular domain, such as education, could be a member. The French ministers did not hide the objective of their government with respect to Quebec. If Canada could not accept the French position, then the Agence would not be established at this Conference, and in a year or two France would establish its own Francophonie, presumably with Quebec participating. Jurgensen then said he would be willing to ask Paris for a phrase that would indicate that any government adhering to the Agence must be authorized to do so by the government on which it depended for foreign affairs. He also said that this was the final position of the French government.

Faced with these hardball tactics, the Canadian delegation engaged in four days of negotiations in search of a compromise. They were at a clear disadvantage because, while the French did not want the Agence and did not care if it failed to materialize, Canada did want it because it represented one of the country's main internal dimensions and was part of the government's bilingual and bicultural policies.

This book is not the place for a blow by blow account of these negotiations. Suffice to say that a compromise was reached, not very different from Jurgensen's final position. This compromise stated that: "Participating governments in full respect of the sovereignty and international competence of all member states, could be admitted as participants in the institutions, activities and programmes of the Agence with the approval of the member state on whose territory the participating government exercises its authority and under terms agreed between the member state and the participating government."[6] In other words, if Ottawa agreed, Quebec would become a participating government in the Agence Francophone. This compromise permitted the French to say that they had obtained membership for Quebec in the Agence. It also permitted Quebec to claim that it had, as a participating government in an international institution, acquired aspects of an international personality. Finally, Ottawa could state that Canada, as a member of the Agence, had fully safeguarded its position of sovereignty in international affairs.

We in Paris were less than enthusiastic about the compromise inasfar as it affected Franco-Canadian relations. In a telegram we pointed out that the Elysée, the Quai D'Orsay and the Paris press considered the compromise a French victory. In one sense we were inclined to agree. It seemed to us that the most important result of Niamey was the recognition by both France and Canada that in certain circumstances, Quebec could have its own international personality within an international francophone agreement. Despite our protests, expressed by the Prime Minister on down, and our hope that the Elysée would not permit De Lipkowski and company to carry on their activities to the end, the French government had maintained its hard position and their Quebec activists could claim that this policy had been successful. We could therefore expect that the policy of duality would be maintained. This did not mean that France would not try to normalize relations with Ottawa during the Sharp and Fanton visits, but it would continue to have the option, subject to conditions in Canada and any requests for aid from Quebec, to revert to De Gaulle's policy of supporting Quebec independence. The possibility of French intervention in our internal affairs remained after Niamey, and so would our task of trying to convince the French of the dangers of such a policy to the French Fact in North America.

NOTES

1. External Affairs Telegram to Embassy Paris, PDF 65, January 21, 1970.
2. Embassy Abidjan Telegram to Ottawa, no. 61, January 26, 1970.
3. Embassy Paris Telegram to Ottawa, no. 523, February 24, 1970.
4. External Affairs Telegram to Embassy Paris, GEU 232, February 27, 1970.
5. Embassy Paris Telegram to Ottawa, no. 631, March 6, 1970.
6. Can. Del. Niamey to Ottawa, no. 40, March 20, 1970.

16

FIRST STEPS TOWARD NORMALIZATION
MITCHELL SHARP VISITS PARIS

THREE EVENTS during April 1970 led to a measure of normalization in relations between France and Canada, without changing the basic duality of French policy. The first was the private visit to Paris of Mitchell Sharp, the Secretary of State for External Affairs, to open the new Canadian Cultural Centre and to have discussions with the French Foreign Minister Maurice Schumann. The second related to the conditions under which the Cultural Agreement between France and Canada should or should not be extended for another five years. The third was the Liberal victory in the Quebec provincial election, which saw the disappearance of the Union Nationale as a political force and the arrival on the scene of the separatist Parti Québécois, a new menace to the Canadian federation.

Mitchell Sharp's visit to Paris of April 1-4, 1970 provided the opportunity for the French government to play up the "normalization" angle of its policy toward Canada. That it fully intended to do so was evident when I arrived at the airport to meet Sharp, for I discovered that Schumann was also there to meet his colleague and accompany him to his hotel. A nice gesture, but French policy remained as ambiguous as ever. We pointed out to Sharp the following item that had appeared in the Paris press after the meeting of the French Cabinet the previous day: "Schumann asserted that the Niamey Conference had recorded the adherence of the Francophone African States and Canada to the Agence Francophone, while the door was left open for an eventual entry of Quebec."

The visit of the minister responsible for foreign affairs fully extends the capacities of an embassy and this visit was no exception. While the two main events were talks between the two Ministers and the opening of the Cultural Centre, Sharp also gave interviews on radio and television, attended the opening of the French National Assembly, visited the Quebec Delegation, saw André Fontaine, editor of the newspaper *Le Monde*, and gave a press conference. My wife arranged a lunch at the Ambassador's residence, presided over by Sharp and attended by two French Ministers, Michelet (Culture) and Giscard D'Estaing (Finance) and various senior bankers and businessmen. She also arranged a dinner for the same day at our residence, so that senior members of the Embassy and their wives could meet their Minister.

In regular meetings that had taken place since 1964 between the French and Canadian Foreign Ministers, at the UN or at NATO, it had been the custom to discuss foreign affairs questions of the moment first. This order of discussion created an ambience which made it somewhat easier to pursue the difficult bilateral matters which followed. The same procedure was followed on this occasion, and we spent a morning on such questions as Vietnam, the Middle East and economic and political relations between the European Common Market and North America. We were interested to see who would accompany Schumann and found him surrounded by Alphand, the Secretary General, De Beaumarchais, the Political Director, Jurgensen, and lesser lights dealing with Canadian-France relations. At the end of the table, by himself, was Léo Hamon, the official spokesperson for President Pompidou, whose assiduous note-taking clearly showed he was under instructions to report on the meeting to the President. There was no sign of De Lipkowski or his advisers. Sharp was accompanied by Paul Tremblay, the new Associate Undersecretary of State for External Affairs, my former Ambassador in Belgium, John Halstead, now Head of European Division, and by myself.

Before the meeting started Schumann took Sharp aside for a private word. This was to the effect that both he and President Pompidou himself were agreed that they did not want to intervene in Canadian affairs in any way. That was their policy, and he was telling Sharp man to man that France wanted good relations with Canada. The Canadian Minister thought this was a clear signal to bear in mind when assessing future French actions. [1] His more battered and cynical civil servants in Paris were inclined to take a "wait and see" attitude.

Mitchell Sharp had always been able to bring an atmosphere of calm reason to the most difficult negotiation, and this occasion was no exception. In his opening remarks he reminded Schumann of his statement to the French National Assembly that France-Quebec cooperation was not incompatible with good Franco-Canadian relations. Since then certain French actions had thrown doubt on French intentions. The most important of these actions was French behaviour at the Second Niamey

Conference. The outcome had been reasonably satisfactory, in that the agreement had been signed by sovereign states who controlled participation of subsidiary governments. It would have been preferable if the agreement had made no mention of subsidiary governments. What concerned Canada was that the French made proposals, at the last minute, to amend the draft constitution of the Agence Francophone. These changes went beyond what had been agreed between Ottawa and Quebec and were put forward in spite of representations made by the Prime Minister of Canada to the President of France. Schumann admitted that France had, all along, wanted non-sovereign states (Quebec) to be admitted, but knew it could not be done without the agreement of sovereign states. But it was done now and there was no point in going back.

Sharp responded by pointing out that the draft constitution had not envisaged non-state membership when Canada was invited to Niamey. French action had inserted a matter of internal jurisdiction into an international conference. As we saw it, a foreign government was supporting the international pretensions of a provincial government in Canada and was therefore intervening in internal Canadian affairs. Schumann, clearly uncomfortable, merely said France did not want to and would not interfere in our affairs.

The Canadian Minister then turned to the Cultural Agreement between France and Canada which was up for renewal in November unless denounced by one of the parties six months in advance. We had therefore until the following month, May, to decide our position. Canada had no problems with the Agreement itself but there had been differences of opinion in the past because of inadequate consultation on major new programs of France-Quebec cooperation, such as space satellites. Ottawa could not admit that a provincial government could deal with a foreign government without the approval of Ottawa. Sharp also referred to French ministerial visits, which should be based on international practice, not on a French interpretation of the Cultural Agreement it had with Quebec. It was incompatible with such practice, and with normal courtesy, that French ministers like De Lipkowski should pay official visits to Quebec without asking leave of the Canadian government. Canada wanted in the future to discuss such visits with French authorities before they were made. Schumann reverted to the French interpretation of the Cultural Agreement as it covered visits such as De Lipkowski's to Quebec. There was considerable argument about different interpretations of the Cultural Agreements, and the actual French policy was smoked out when Schumann claimed that these agreements did not give Ottawa a *droit de regard* over developments in France-Quebec cooperation: so much for the professed intention not to interfere in Canada's internal affairs. Sharp responded by stating that we could not accept a situation in which Ottawa had nothing to say about either French visits to Quebec or major new programs of France-Quebec cooperation.

At the end of the session Sharp summed up the Canadian attitude as follows. Good relations between France and Canada implied three things: France-Quebec cooperation must be carried out in consultation with Canadian federal authorities; France-Canada cooperation must be a matter not only of words but also of concrete proposals from each side; France must abstain from gestures that were contrary to the federal government's constitutional position. Schumann said he agreed with the first two points; as for the third, he reiterated that France did not want to and would not interfere in Canadian affairs.

After the meeting Hamon told Tremblay that he had been impressed both by Sharp's able and very frank presentation of the Canadian position and by the evident spirit of cooperation that had presided over the meeting. He wished us to know that we could expect an "inflexion" in French policy toward Canada. This word can be interpreted as either "a bend from a direct line" or "a change in direction." I was inclined to the first interpretation but then I had, perhaps, been too long in Paris.

The inauguration of the Cultural Centre was attended by some eight hundred guests, including leading figures from the cultural world in Canada and France, and a sizeable contingent from the press. That it was such a success was largely due to a remarkable speech by Léo Hamon, who spoke of Franco-Canadian relations with a warmth that we had not heard in the last decade. He told us later that he had been appalled by the draft he had received from the Quai D'Orsay and had spent an evening writing his own version. An excerpt will give the tone:

One misunderstands Canada if one regards it simply as a French culture and a British culture living side by side but strangers to each other. Those who speak English would not be at home in Canada if they did not live in proximity to those who speak French and vice versa. It is thus the juxtaposition and the overlapping of these two cultures that give Canada the specificity that is its own. Yours is a country that is only itself because it is diverse. You represent the richness and originality of a country in the New World which intends to remain itself despite the mass and power of your southern neighbour, a country that can only remain true to itself by preserving its diversity.

At the opening of the Canadian Cultural Centre in Paris, April 1970. Léo Hamon, spokesman for President Pompidou (left), is talking with the author.

I could only wonder, on listening to these words, how many Canadians of the two cultures saw it this way.[2]

Our assessment of the visit was that despite its private nature it had effectively reinforced the Canadian presence in France. Sharp had clearly laid out the Canadian position on principal differences between France and Canada to his French opposite number, in the presence of a representative of the French President. The next set of priorities comprised the renewal of the Cultural Agreement with France, conditions for ministerial visits and the establishment of cooperative programs, particularly in the fields of science and technology, to give substance to an improved era in our relations with France. What Sharp accomplished was a preliminary but essential step toward renewing regular dialogue with France. Conditions seemed propitious, but what was missing was an appropriate Ambassador to conduct this dialogue at a high level with French politicians, civil servants, parliamentarians and journalists.[3]

In his report to the House of Commons on his return, Sharp emphasized the categorical statement by Schumann that France had no intention of interfering in Canadian internal affairs. He also told the House that, in view of that declaration, any differences arising in future should be easier to resolve.[4] In view of their previous track record, I personally doubted that the French would necessarily keep their word; much depended on the outcome of the forthcoming Quebec election. If the new Quebec government continued to ask France for help in achieving an international personality, then the Gaullists would respond.

NOTES

1. Embassy Paris Telegram to Ottawa, no. 940, April 4, 1970.
2. Embassy Paris Telegram to Ottawa, no. 926, April 3, 1970.
3. Embassy Paris Telegram to Ottawa, no. 991, April 8, 1970.
4. House of Commons, *Debates*, 5665-5666, April 9, 1970.

17

RENEWAL OF THE FRANCO-CANADIAN CULTURAL AGREEMENT
AND THE QUEBEC ELECTION

IF CANADA WAS TO TAKE ACTION on the renewal of the Cultural Agreement with France, it had to do so by May 17, 1970 at the latest. On his return from France Mitchell Sharp had a memorandum prepared for the Prime Minister, setting out various options that the Canadian government could choose, as well as a recommendation, which Trudeau approved on April 29, the day of the Quebec election.[1] These options are worth examining, for they illustrate the complexity of the three-cornered Ottawa-Quebec-Paris relationship. They were all based on the assumption, confirmed by Sharp's trip to Paris, that France would not change its policy in the short term to meet the requirements of the federal government. The Agreement itself provided the framework for all Franco-Canadian cultural exchanges, was of particular importance to Francophones outside Quebec, and also created the constitutional and political framework for the Agreements between France and Quebec.

The options were as follows:

- *A Simple Renewal of the Agreement without Conditions*
  This course would mean accepting the climate of ambiguity that had existed between Ottawa and Paris since the original signing of the Agreement in 1965. It would also provide justification for all the abuses of interpretation of the Agreement committed by both France and Quebec during that period.

- *Formal Termination of the Agreement*
  This action would eliminate all the formal structures that provided the basis for cultural relations between the two countries. It would not eliminate France-Quebec cultural cooperation; instead, it would leave the field open to Quebec and France to do what they wished. Such action would also encourage Quebec to claim it had an international personality in the cultural area and that it was therefore "sovereign" in international matters within its jurisdiction.

- *Termination and Renegotiation*
  Neither the time nor the necessary conditions existed for such a negotiation. France could drag out negotiations, even if it agreed to enter into them, until the expiry of the Agreement six months later.
- *Offer to Renegotiate*
  Here too, time was not available. Canada would find itself obliged either to renounce the Agreement or to renew it with a unilateral interpretation, which the French would refuse or more likely ignore.
- *Renounce the Agreement but Propose Negotiations on the Documents Annexed to the Agreement*
  It was difficult to see why the French would accept that the Agreement could be renewed but that the Exchange of Letters permitting the conclusion of arrangements with the provinces should be renegotiated. This would be asking the French to admit that cultural relations with Ottawa were more important to them than arrangements with the provinces and in particular with Quebec.
- *Renewal of the Agreement together with a Formal Explanation of the Significance for Canada of this Renewal*
  This approach would also include an offer by Canada that any differences in interpreting the Agreement should be the subject of bilateral consultations. This option was presented to the Prime Minister as the least bad choice, given the circumstances. It had the advantage of renewing the Agreement while at the same time giving Canada the opportunity to officially set out its interpretation of both the Agreement and the Annexed Letters. This would not be a unilateral interpretation since we were offering at the same time to negotiate any differences of interpretation.

Ottawa thought that such an approach would face France with four choices: to terminate the Agreement, which seemed unlikely in view of its own stated policy of assisting Francophone culture in North America; to agree to the Canadian explanation, also unlikely in view of its policy of duality; to offer its own interpretation of the Agreement, to which we could reply that it was up to Canada to interpret the meaning of the Agreement but that we should be pleased to consult the French on their interpretation; not to reply at all and let matters develop until the next major disagreement. It was this course that we thought the French would follow, for it committed them to nothing new, while permitting them to say to the ultra-Gaullists that there had been no change in French policy.

We had no illusions that renewal would end the political differences between the three parties, but it would have the advantage of placing the federal government on a firmer legal basis and forcing the French to take a more defensive posture than in the past. They would now find it more difficult to claim unilaterally that a particular action on their part was in conformity with either their own or Quebec's interpretation of the Canadian constitution.

The Cultural Agreement between France and Quebec was also due for renewal within the same time frame. To cover all the bases, and emphasize the sovereign right of the federal government to conduct foreign policy, it was decided that, in explaining our interpretation of the agreement to the French and Quebec governments, we should make it clear that this interpretation also applied to all agreements between France and Quebec, including the Agreement on Education.

In approving the sixth option, the Prime Minister agreed that Sharp should call in the French Ambassador before 17 May to present and explain our note, and send a further note, a few days later, on the France-Quebec Agreement. In addition, it was agreed that since Quebec was clearly an interested party, it should be informed of Ottawa's note at the same time as the French. The election of the Bourassa government brought a change in how Ottawa intended to proceed, though not in the decision to renew the Cultural Agreement or in the Canadian explanation of its reasons for doing so. There was concern in Ottawa that its action on the Agreement right after the Quebec election would be misinterpreted in Quebec, so the note was revised to remove any implication that Ottawa's concerns with French behaviour were the result of abuses by Quebec. The game plan was changed, and Trudeau first sent a personal and confidential letter to Premier Bourassa explaining why Ottawa thought it necessary to make certain points clear to the French government at this particular time. A few days later a more formal letter explaining Ottawa's intentions was sent to the provinces, including Quebec.[2]

Finally, on 11 May, Sharp called in the French Ambassador.[3] The latter, having rapidly read the note which Sharp handed to him, expatiated at length (as ambassadors are wont to do) on the French position as outlined by Maurice Schumann during Sharp's visit to Paris. He ended, like Schumann, by declaring that if the Canadian government sought the right to control fundamentals of any agreement between France and Canada, this was a new element that could lead to serious problems. Sharp replied by referring to the spirit of the text of the Agreement, and told the Ambassador that the lesson he drew from recent Franco-Canadian relations was not that France sought to create difficulties for Canada, but that certain elements within the French and Quebec governments had used France-Quebec cooperation to promote the acquisition by Quebec of international status. It had become evident that France had served as a means to promote the cause of international status for Quebec. This was something Ottawa could never accept, hence the Canadian explanations in the note, so that France would not find itself mixed up in Canadian internal affairs.

At this point, the Minister told the Ambassador that Premier Bourassa had been informed in advance of the contents of the note by the Prime Minister. Bourassa had expressed his appreciation and replied that his priorities were elsewhere: he was interested in substance not form; he hoped to reinforce federalism and intended to conduct relations with France in that spirit. Sharp went on to call the Ambassador's attention to two points: that all French-speaking Canadians should profit from cooperation between the two countries and that Anglophone provinces should not be neglected, though they understood the particular need to preserve French culture in Canada. He repeated Ottawa's belief in Franco-Canadian cooperation but emphasized that it must not be used as a vehicle for separatism. In reply, the Ambassador referred to a recent press conference by Schumann, where he had pointed out that French support for French-speaking Canadians was not to be confused with support for separatism: it was possible for French Canada to expand within the Canadian federal system. The Ambassador asked the precise reason for Canada's suggestion in the note that there be consultations whenever there was a disagreement on the interpretation of the Agreement. Sharp responded by saying that Canada believed the Agreement should be renewed but that any time there seemed to be a need to interpret the Agreement Canada, for its part, was willing to do so. [4]

The last stage in this development took place two weeks later, when the two Foreign Ministers lunched together during the NATO Spring Ministerial Meeting in Rome. The French were quite explicit in indicating that they would make greater efforts to harmonize France-Quebec relations with Franco-Canadian relations, and that they expected this task to be easier in light of the Quebec election. Sharp explained that the purpose of the recent note was not to put the substance of the Cultural Agreement in question but to resolve any future divergences through mutual consultation. Canada was not suggesting a formal review of the

Agreement, but consultations as the need arose. Schumann said that France had not replied to our note, nor did he say when or whether there would be an explicit reply. He implied that France was happy with things as they were, and Sharp agreed that divergences were more unlikely as a result of the election of the new Quebec government. The previous government had tried to establish a separate international personality but that question had been settled, at least in part, by the election. The new government would be concentrating on getting a better deal within the federation, which would make things more difficult for Ottawa but should make Franco-Canadian relations easier.

Schumann could not leave well enough alone and reverted, somewhat clumsily, to the French policy of duality. He said that France was governed by two basic principles in its relations with Canada: first, that the France-Quebec "ententes should be kept alive and in their present form in accordance with the Canadian constitution as interpreted by Quebec as a party to the ententes"; second, "that France had no desire to weaken the Canadian federation." In other words, Schumann was saying that France's relations with Canada depended on the policy of the Quebec government in power at the time. With a federalist party newly elected all was well, but if another party should come to power, such as the separatists, France was reserving its position.

Sharp quite naturally took issue with the statement that it was for Quebec to interpret the Canadian constitution to France. There were two parties in international law to these ententes, France and Canada, and it was the approval of the federal government that gave the France-Quebec ententes their international validity. Interpretations of the constitution might be a matter for discussion between Ottawa and the provinces, but it was for the federal government alone to interpret the Canadian constitution to foreign governments. Schumann remarked that this was an interesting legal theory that need not be invoked, since relations with Ottawa were satisfactory. Here was further proof, if proof was required, that this French government intended to retain an option with regard to its future actions respecting Ottawa and Quebec. [5]

Outside the field of direct Franco-Canadian relations, Sharp gave Schumann his interpretation of the Quebec election results, which is interesting in itself, as it represented the views and hopes of a senior Canadian Minister of the Trudeau government some months before the tragic events leading to the October Crisis in 1970. Sharp believed that the previous Quebec government had, in part, been defeated because it had been divided within itself, and because it had wasted its energies on constitutional and prestige issues that did not touch the people's standard of living. The new Premier was an able and down-to-earth man who emphasized bread and butter issues. He was a convinced federalist but he could be expected to bargain hard to improve Quebec's lot within the federation. He would be straightforward in his relations with France and also with Ottawa. He had to succeed.

The Liberal victory in the Quebec election certainly changed, at least for the time being, the nature of Franco-Canadian relations, but the arrival in force of the separatist Parti Québécois (PQ), with 23 percent of the vote, raised questions that have yet to be answered about the future of the Canadian federation. The size of the Liberal victory certainly surprised the French government and press. What had been expected was a narrow Union Nationale win or, more likely, a minority Union Nationale or Liberal government, with the newly arrived Parti Québécois sufficiently strong to make it difficult for the minority government to function. The reaction in Paris was varied. There were no reactions official or unofficial from the French government. Our old adversary Jurgensen claimed he had expected a narrow Liberal win, did not think the essentials of our relationship would change, and preferred to wait until things settled down. In any case, it was clear that the Quai would have to behave somewhat differently than it had done in the past for, as Jurgensen himself said, he knew only one or two elected Liberals. The French press commented widely on the election: some saw in it a new stability, due to the victory of a federalist party; others detected a new and unsettling mortgage on the future of the federation because of the impressive strength of the PQ vote. The government-controlled radio and television systems remained as Gaullist as ever, concentrating their reporting on the success of the PQ, attributed largely to the "Vive le Québec libre" speech of General De Gaulle.

The Embassy reaction was that the total silence of the French government was hardly surprising, as they must be uncertain about future tactics and they had few Quebec guides, since most of their allies and contacts had disappeared. They would now have to establish links with the new Bourassa government and learn for themselves how it intended to treat relations with France. Meanwhile, fate had so arranged it that the next series of events would accentuate the importance of relations with federal institutions. The two Foreign Ministers met in Rome, the French Secretary of State for Defence was to visit Ottawa and Canadian Armed

Secretary of State for Defence was to visit Ottawa and Canadian Armed Forces bases, and a Canadian parliamentary delegation was expected in Paris for the annual meeting of the Franco-Canadian Parliamentary Association.

This chapter concludes with a story illustrating how out of touch the federal and Quebec civil servants in Paris were with events in Canada, preoccupied as they were with the seemingly endless feuds between Ottawa, Paris and Quebec. The Quebec Delegation expected a Union Nationale win or a minority government with a strong separatist element in the Quebec Assembly, and they prepared to celebrate the occasion with the members of the French "Quebec Mafia." A large reception was arranged and the champagne was ready. As the results came in faces became longer and longer, guests started to drift away, and the champagne remained corked. At the Embassy we decided to run a sweepstake, with the person closest to the final result taking all. With one exception, all the participants predicted some form of Union Nationale win or Liberal minority government. The exception, who predicted a Liberal majority win was, somewhat embarrassingly, an Anglophone, namely myself. I hasten to add that I too was far off the actual seat count. What to do with my ill-gotten gains to ensure good morale? I gave my winnings to the organizers of our annual Christmas children's party so that they could bring in a delightful marionnette show from the Park in the Champs Elysées.

NOTES

1. Memorandum to Prime Minister from Secretary of State for External Affairs, April 28, 1970.
2. Memorandum to Prime Minister from Secretary of State for External Affairs, May 6, 1970.
3. External Affairs Telegram to Embassy Paris, GEU 608, May 11, 1970.
4. External Affairs Telegram to Embassy Paris, GEU 612, May 12, 1970.
5. Embassy Rome Telegram to Ottawa, no. 594, May 12, 1970.

18

A NEW AMBASSADOR—THE OCTOBER CRISIS—THE END OF AN ERA

THE SPRING AND SUMMER of 1970 saw the commencement of a return to more normal relations between France and Canada, with respect to ministerial visits and to behaviour toward Canadian representatives in Paris. The process culminated in the autumn with the arrival of a new Ambassador who had, until his appointment, been a member of the Trudeau government.

The first step was the visit at the end of May of Fanton, the French Secretary of State for Defence, an indication on the part of the French that one of their ministers, albeit a junior one in an area of undisputed federal jurisdiction, could visit Ottawa. The important requirement was that the visit should be seen to take place without incident and in a relaxed atmosphere. Fanton's host was Léo Cadieux, the Canadian Minister of Defence, who was shortly to be named Ambassador to France. There were no incidents and Fanton was particularly impressed by the NORAD Command Centre at North Bay and the new École Militaire at St. Jean. Some small areas of cooperation between the two armed forces were expanded, primarily in regard to the exchange of officers, training, and the process of bilingualization then taking place in the Canadian Forces.

Not everything changed at once; for example, De Lipkowski continued to do silly things that embarrassed his government as much as ourselves. Delivering a speech at the first meeting of the administrative council of the Agence Francophone he managed to mention all participants, including Quebec—save one—Canada, which was providing 30 percent of the budget. He then excused himself to the Canadian representative in front of a representative from Schumann's office, who could only say to the Canadian, *sotto voce*, that this lapse was regrettable, indeed, unbelievable. Fortunately this was the last time De Lipkowski appeared on the Canadian scene.

Other events during that summer contributed to a general relaxation. Robert Stanfield, the Leader of the Opposition, came to Paris and saw

Schumann. He was particularly helpful in stressing to the French Minister that his party too believed in normal Franco-Canadian relations and cooperative arrangements between France and all parts of Canada. He was also the first senior Canadian to raise with a French minister the problem that would face Canada when the United Kingdom's entry into the European Economic Community would bring about the disappearance of Commonwealth preferences. This subject would have its part to play in Franco-Canadian relations in a few years' time. Gérard Pelletier was also back, to attend the inaugural Festival of Film in the French Language in the company of Quebec and French ministerial colleagues. This was the first time since my arrival in Paris that three ministers of the triangular relationship had attended an international event in a relaxed manner and without dispute. The only conflict that arose was among the film-makers, with the Africans and Canadians banding together against what they saw as French cultural imperialism.

The treatment accorded to the Canadian Embassy staff in Paris improved during the year. General De Gaulle had given orders, after his return from Montreal in 1967, that within the French bureaucracy the staff of the Canadian Embassy in Paris should be kept at arms' length and dealt with officially through the traditional channels of the Quai D'Orsay. In my various trips outside Paris, the effect of this edict had been particularly noticeable, except in places where the mayor or the Deputy was from an anti-Gaullist Party. That there had been a change in orders first came to our attention when I visited Lille to attend a Canadian Day at the local fair, a month after Sharp's visit to Paris. When I arrived, the official atmosphere, instead of being cold and formal, was suddenly full of friendship and courtesy. The local Deputy, Pierre Billecocq, was Secretary of State for Education, and he incorporated me as guest of honour at a banquet for the representatives of the regional universities and educational institutions, and insisted that I give a speech. He also arranged for me to give an interview to the Lille press and to appear on television. This attention was all the more unusual in that Billecocq had been one of two French ministers who had confronted Gérard Pelletier at the Niamey Conference only two months previously, with the French "take it or leave it" position on Quebec's participation in the Agence Francophone.

Later that summer I attended a similar occasion at Caen in Normandy, where we had always been warmly received, despite General De Gaulle, because of the valiant efforts of the Canadian army during the invasion and liberation of Normandy in 1944. A few days before my departure a message was received from the Prefect, the representative of Paris in the local administration, asking me to stay with him during my visit and saying he was organizing a large dinner in my honour to be attended by all the deputies of Normandy and their wives. The piquant aspect of this offer (which I naturally accepted), was that the arrangements for my visit were in the hands of an official of the Prefect's office, a Canadian from the Department of External Affairs finishing his year at the French National School of Administration. It was rather delightful, after all that had happened, to find one Canadian Foreign Service Officer taking charge of the official visit of another to the administrative centre of a French *département.*

The next step forward in regularizing French ministerial visits to Canada was notification by the French that their Secretary of State for the Civil Service, Philippe Malaud, was to visit Quebec and that he would accept an invitation to Ottawa if it were offered. This approach had been worked out by the French and ourselves on the basis that the launching of the Bilingualization Program in the Federal Civil Service would make his visit opportune. His advice could be useful and he would be able to report to his President on the seriousness of Ottawa's policy in this domain. Ottawa did invite him, and then the visit nearly fell apart when the French discovered that Prime Minister Trudeau would be receiving Jean-Jacques Servan-Schreiber on the same day Malaud would be visiting Ottawa. This political journalist was the editor of *L'Express* (the French equivalent of *Time* magazine) and had arrogated to himself the position of leader of the non-Communist opposition; he was therefore anathema to President Pompidou.

To avoid yet another incident involving the Canadian prime minister and a visiting French minister, we informed the French that Trudeau particularly wished to see Malaud, as he had a letter for personal delivery to President Pompidou. In actual fact, Trudeau saw Malaud in Montreal, while his reception of Servan-Schreiber was turned into a private luncheon without publicity. The purpose of the letter was to introduce the new Canadian Ambassador to France, Léo Cadieux, at that time Minister of National Defence, and to explain to President Pompidou the importance that Trudeau attached to Cadieux's mission in France, coming as it did at the beginning of a new phase in relations between the two countries.

On many occasions during the past two years our visitors from Canada had quizzed me about what sort of person I envisaged as the next ambassador to France. My reply was always the same: first, Franco-

Canadian relations had to be returning to normal, and as long as France continued an active policy of duality it was best to make no change. When the day came, as it would, that normality was a French as well as a Canadian objective, we should, in my opinion (contrary to the normal feelings of a career foreign service officer) send a political ambassador, preferably one who had been a member of the Trudeau Cabinet. Such a choice would of course flatter the French, but more importantly, a person of this kind could engage in dialogue at the political as well as the senior bureaucratic levels, provided he was sympathetic and knew his France. His objective, quite apart from continuing the normalization of relations, would be to find areas where Canada and France could cooperate and work together, in addition to the important but always tricky subjects of culture, education and language.

The choice of Léo Cadieux could not have been better. He had the personality and the credentials to fill the post. He had been a war correspondent in London during World War II, had founded one of the first reviews of French literature in Quebec and, as editor, had visited France every year; he was a Pearsonian, not a Trudeau Liberal, the only one besides Mitchell Sharp, in the first self-absorbed Trudeau Cabinet, to fight against those who either wished to remove Canadian troops from Europe or to get out of NATO altogether. His common sense and political experience were to establish him, in a short period, as the authentic spokesperson for Canada in Paris. I knew we were in for a pleasant change when he arrived at the airport. He was greeted by a troop of French and Canadian journalists whose questions he answered, managing to weave into every one an appropriate quotation from a French writer or poet.

Maurice Schumann went out of his way to greet Cadieux, claiming that he remembered him from London days when Schumann had been De Gaulle's spokesperson. Cadieux was quite sure they had never met but if Schumann wanted it that way, why not? Their first official meeting was almost effusive in its friendliness, with Schumann asserting that all the misunderstandings were now dissipated and that it was most flattering for France that the Canadian government had sent someone from an important ministry to represent the country in Paris. Both men went through the list of our differences along the lines of the last meeting between Schumann and Sharp, with Schumann repeating that he did not believe in the sovereignty option and that federalism was the only realistic formula.

Some of Cadieux's remarks are worth noting, for they represented a view of Franco-Canadian relations that has not fundamentally changed over the years. Cadieux told the Foreign Minister that the Canadian government wished the complete re-establishment of the conditions that had previously existed—meaning before De Gaulle—between the two countries. The Trudeau government, like the Pearson government before it, was engaged in an internal policy vital to the survival of the country. This policy was to install, in Canada, wherever it proved necessary, a regime of official bilingualism within federal institutions. This policy presented a challenge that France could not ignore because of its own desire to maintain the French language and culture. Canadian interest in La Francophonie was a justified prolongation of this internal policy and it was in the interest of both countries that their policies should be complementary, rather than competitive. Cadieux considered his appointment represented a belief on the part of Ottawa that a new start could be made in our relations that would favour honest dialogue rather than some of the ambiguous abstractions of the last few years.[1]

It is interesting to compare these words with the assessment that had been prepared by External Affairs at this same time for Sharp, suggesting how Ottawa might take advantage of the new climate to achieve a more realistic balance in the federal government's relations with France. The departure of De Gaulle and the defeat of the Union Nationale government had certainly modified the relationship for the better, but there were still negative elements that had to be taken into account, such as the continuing strong Gaullist influence within the French government, the rising separatist movement in Quebec, and the complete separation between Franco-Canadian and France-Quebec cooperation. The impulse given by De Gaulle to French policy still existed, and while the style and even the content had improved, a fundamental area of disagreement remained: namely, France's policy of duality between Ottawa and Quebec. This would not alter for the foreseeable future, unless the unexpected happened, such as a further change of government in France or a new constitutional agreement that permitted a more stable relationship between Quebec and the rest of Canada. We would therefore have to live with a certain ambiguity in the relationship, which did not mean that we should not take advantage of the current improvement in relations to search out practical areas of cooperation with France. This would be a slow process, given the distrust of French policy that had accumulated in Canada over the past three years and the bitterness existing in the Ottawa bureaucracy as a result of continual French interference in the Canadian domestic scene.

As had been the case from the start of the Quiet Revolution, the best method for ensuring a minimum of French interference was the promotion of cooperation between Ottawa and the Quebec government. As long as France could not claim that in a particular instance Quebec had asked for French assistance, then relations should remain relatively stable. Even so, it had to be accepted that the Pompidou regime, at least, would never completely support a federalist Canada—even if they claimed that it was the only future for the country—as long as there was the possibility of a separatist government coming to power in Quebec which might require the assistance of France.

The Department of External Affairs recommended once again to Sharp that we maintain the policy we had followed since 1967: on the one hand, openness to all forms of cooperation with France; on the other, firmness when France attempted to interfere in Canadian domestic affairs. It was also wise to maintain a favourable public image in France in order to make it more difficult politically for the Gaullists to return to their previous practices. In this respect recent events and the new Ambassador would help. The advice was sound if not original, and showed that Ottawa had a clear appreciation of the degree of trustworthiness of Pompidou's Gaullist government.[2]

The positive turn in our relations with France was confirmed when Léo Cadieux presented his Letters of Credence to President Pompidou on October 16. As the one person who had been present at both Beaulieu's presentation to De Gaulle and this one, I was able to compare the atmosphere of the two events. The first took place at freezing point, the second had the temperature of a warm spring day. The statisticians at the Embassy told us that the Beaulieu presentation lasted twelve minutes and this one twenty-six minutes, so we were definitely moving in the right direction: no problems this time about photographers or press releases.

The conversation between the two men was relaxed and cordial. They were two practical politicians, neither given to Gaullist grandeur. Pompidou's main message was that Canada could count on the full cooperation of members of his government without any shadows from the past. At this point Maurice Schumann smiled his most seductive smile and nodded his head. It was clear from the President's words that, as we had anticipated, the nomination of a member of the Trudeau Cabinet had been appreciated as a sign of amity.

The President raised three specific points: French investments in Canada were insufficient, but he hoped that his policy of opening up the

Ambassador Léo Cadieux and the author are received by the French Chief of Protocol (left), on the occasion of the presentation of Letters of Credence to President Pompidou. October 16, 1970.

French economy and turning away from years of protectionism would educate French business leaders to change their habits; and bilingualism was a formula that France herself applied or at least should apply. Following this rather extraordinary remark the President suggested that Canada could help France by furnishing young Anglophones to teach English. We never did get to the bottom of this suggestion—presumably he was trying to indicate his approval for the policy of bilingualism. We did not expect to live to see the day when young Canadian Anglophones would officially be teaching English in French *lycées*. The third point was the need for both countries to share their experience and complement their efforts in the field of development aid, particularly in Francophone countries. This referred to the fact that the same week, the first of what were to become annual consultations between the aid organizations of France and Canada was taking place in Paris.[3]

As we were leaving after the ceremony, Schumann whispered in the Ambassador's ear an unexpected question, "How is your Prime Minister?" To the response "Fine, thank you," he said, "We await you, we await you." This seemed to be a hint that a Trudeau visit would now be welcome, which we doubted. The Ambassador followed up the suggestion on a suitable occasion, and from Schumann's embarrassed change of subject it became clear that the Foreign Minister had been carried away by the euphoria of the moment. In fact, it would take four more years and another change of president before Pierre Trudeau would officially set foot on French soil.

The day after the presentation, my wife and I left on a trip to the south of France, a badly needed break for us both after the stresses and strains of the past year. The next morning, in the depths of Burgundy, we turned on the radio to hear that Pierre Laporte had been murdered and that a self-styled FLQ cell in Paris had made threats against the Ambassador and his family. While we knew that the French would provide full security for the Ambassador and the Embassy, might there not be a risk to the family of the Anglophone deputy? Should we return? After much phoning, the laying on of precautions by the Embassy, and a conversation with our eldest daughter, we were encouraged to continue. It was a wonderful trip but there was always a worry in the background. We consoled ourselves with the thought that no stranger would ever get by the eagle eye of our remarkably disagreeable concierge.

President Pompidou made a statement on events in Quebec the day after the murder and two days after the Ambassador had presented his credentials. He utterly condemned the assassination and all similar acts of violence, particularly when the victims were hostages. He also expressed the preoccupation of France with the effect these events could have on "the French Fact in Canada." His initial remarks were from a man who had not forgotten the semi-revolutionary events of May 1968, and constituted a warning that his administration would not tolerate any terrorist hostage-taking. His statement about "the French Fact in Canada," rather than just in Quebec, was a step away from strict Gaullist orthodoxy and was, we were told, his own personal contribution. All in all, it was a moderate and prudent reaction appropriate to the new era of normalization. [4]

As a practical measure the Embassy and the Residence had armed detachments from the paramilitary forces of the Interior Department stationed outside the premises for the next three or four months. The Ambassador was provided with a bodyguard who turned out to be a poet, and the two men discussed French literature on their daily walks to and from the office. I wondered whether the RCMP had similar capabilities.

The Cross kidnapping and the Laporte murder precipitated a rediscovery of Canada and the future of Quebec by French politicians and the media. At first there was comprehension of the measures taken by the provincial and federal authorities, except at the political extremes. The President of the Parti Socialiste Unifié (PSU), Michel Rocard, who would later, in his more moderate period, become a socialist prime minister, supported the FLQ actions in intransigent revolutionary terms. The Gaullist newspaper *La Nation* and government radio and television revived the events surrounding De Gaulle's "Vive le Québec libre," and his support for an independent Quebec. Many of the French media travelled to Montreal and nowhere else, and once there, became less and less interested in the search for Laporte's murderers and the ongoing Cross kidnapping. Instead they concentrated on the origins of the crisis and the reactions of the population. This led to a great deal of political analysis— a favourite French sport—based on little knowledge of (or interest in) Canadian history—often the upshot of interviews with those who had an axe to grind, such as René Lévesque, always good for a *bon mot* and a headline. The result was a great deal of muddled and contradictory reporting that only added to the confusion evident in French public opinion since De Gaulle's trip to Canada in 1967. One thing, however, was clear to them: the position of Quebec within North America was unsettled and would remain so.

In the midst of all this, General De Gaulle died. He was one of history's flawed heros, whose era and aura did not last beyond his state funeral, though his myths can still be found in the political life of both France and Quebec. His death created the problem of deciding who would represent Canada at the funeral of a man who, depending on your point of view, had so justly or insolently interfered in Canada's domestic affairs. The solution, found after much palaver, was typical but in the circumstances appropriate. Quebec was represented by two senior ministers while the federal government was represented by its Foreign Minister, Mitchell Sharp, and the Ambassador. Since there were no delegations, those attending were seated according to function and there could not be any dispute about who outranked whom. A commemorative mass was held in the Catholic Basilica in Ottawa and attended by Trudeau.

The curtain came down on a year in which some progress had been made in Franco-Canadian relations. Schumann and Sharp met at NATO in December.[5] The Canadian Minister was able to inform his French colleague that there had been a break in the Cross kidnapping, and the latter congratulated the Canadian government on the firm position it had maintained. He also restated the French position that it was essential to demonstrate that kidnapping and blackmail did not pay. Then, letting French duality show itself, Schumann expressed the hope that the federal government was not taking advantage of the situation to reduce the position of the Quebec government. On the contrary, replied Sharp, from the beginning of the crisis Ottawa had maintained that the basic decisions had to be taken by Quebec. Both Ministers agreed that normalization was proceeding well and that the Franco-Canadian Cultural Agreement had in effect been tacitly renewed, and Sharp invited Schumann to pay an official visit to Canada. The French Minister said he would like to come but could not commit himself to a date; his Ambassador in Ottawa followed this up with a tentative suggestion that he come when he attended the autumn session of the United Nations in 1971. Normalization was to continue.

NOTES

1. Embassy Paris Telegram to Ottawa, no. 2994, September 28, 1970.
2. Memorandum to the Secretary of State for External Affairs from the Undersecretary, October 6, 1970.
3. Embassy Paris Telegram to Ottawa, no. 3184, October 19, 1970.
4. Embassy Paris Telegram to Ottawa, no. 3231, October 21, 1970.
5. Can. Del., NATO Telegram to Ottawa, no. 2976, December 4, 1970.

19

NORMALIZATION: BOURASSA VISITS PARIS, SCHUMANN COMES TO OTTAWA

NORMALIZATION OF RELATIONS between Paris and Ottawa was now underway but it was necessary to put substance into these relations in order to widen France's interests in Canada beyond language, culture and education in Quebec and the partially Francophone provinces. Did it matter? Many in the country did not think so, but the Trudeau government saw this objective as an essential component of the policy it was defining for Canada, as a partially Francophone country with a policy of bilingualism and biculturalism, intending to play its part in the Francophone international community while ensuring that France would no longer be tempted to interfere in Canadian domestic affairs. The goal must be to encourage commercial, industrial, technological and scientific links with France.

To create a substantive relationship with France would not be easy, for her priorities were the evolving European Community, Eastern Europe, the African Continent and the Mediterranean littoral. However Canada had a card to play, namely investment in a dynamic and expanding economy, particularly in primary resources, where France already had a stake in oil in Alberta and potash in Saskatchewan. The main stumbling block was Canada's geography: we were the neighbours and the main trading partner of the United States. De Gaulle and his successors were hypnotized by the danger to France and the European Community represented by the American behemoth. The Gaullists argued that helping to maintain French language and culture in Canada was one thing, but a search for closer economic relations with Canada was quite different, since it risked giving the U.S. a side door into protectionist France. There was a fundamental dichotomy in this argument between assistance to French Canadians to better resist assimilation by the English-speaking majority in North America and a refusal of closer economic relations, which could enable Canada to diversify its external economic relationships, on grounds that Canada was a stalking horse for the United States. In today's global economy this view seems even more short-sighted than it did at the time.

The policy of substantive relations with France was no more popular on the Canadian side, where a majority of the business community and the economic bureaucrats in Ottawa believed that the Canadian economy was inevitably attached to that of the U.S., and obtained its protection through such multilateral organizations as the GATT. Given De Gaulle's intervention, why should any particular effort be made to establish a substantive relationship with France, particularly at a time when Canada's other former colonial power, the United Kingdom, was once again negotiating its entry into the European Common Market, and Commonwealth preferences in trade were about to disappear?

The Trudeau government, reacting to recent unilateral actions from Washington (see Chapter 20) started to explore counterbalances to U.S. economic preponderance, such as some form of special relationship with the European Economic Community. Such a policy would require the benevolent understanding of France, more likely to be forthcoming if there was to be new substance to our own bilateral relations.

It is against this background, disturbed from time to time by attempts of Gaullists to create problems, that relations with France should be seen in the next five years, leading up to the Contractual Link between Canada and the European Community in 1976. During this period Quebec concentrated on economic development of the province, including encouragement of French investment, while maintaining the agreements it already had with France in the fields of education, culture and youth exchanges. The separatists within the Quebec bureaucracy continued to have influence, but after the failure of the Victoria Constitutional Charter, the more important among them left to pursue active political careers in the rising Parti Québécois; they nevertheless left behind many disciples to press sovereignty options within the Quebec Civil Service. The latest failure of Canadians to reach constitutional agreement and the growing strength of the PQ did not lead to a return of Gaullist intervention, because by then there was a new French President, Valéry Giscard D'Estaing, less dependent on the Gaullists and therefore less inclined to tell Canadians how to settle their affairs. Under his regime a new ambiguous policy was devised that permitted France to stay out of Canadian quarrels. This policy of "non-ingérence, non-indifférence" (non-interference, non-indifference) has served France well to this day.

At the beginning of the new normalization period in 1971, we realized that one of our best instruments for encouraging Canadian ministers to come up with substantive proposals for cooperation was Léo Cadieux himself, and that the longer he was away from Ottawa and its daily preoccupations the more he would become a wasting asset. It was therefore agreed that, after he had presented his credentials and visited specific French ministers, he would return to Ottawa to report to the Prime Minister, see some of his former colleagues, and visit Premier Bourassa of Quebec and Premier Robarts of Ontario. His most amusing visit had been to De Lipkowski, who after listening to the Ambassador for twenty minutes, evolved from convinced separatist to a believer in special status, and finally to a reasoned pessimism about the future of French-speaking Canadians.

The Ambassador told Prime Minister Trudeau that the fact that he had been a member of the Cabinet had ensured that he had been well received in France and that all doors were now open to him. He had the impression from his meetings there that the French government did not want to be placed in a position where it had to choose between Ottawa and Quebec because, given the political strength of the Gaullists, France would choose Quebec. The Pompidou government was willing to cooperate with Ottawa in areas yet to be defined, but it would be up to Canada to come forward with precise proposals that we would be willing to carry through with despatch. If there was no progress because of our fundamental disinterest or our slowness in putting forward proposals then we should not blame the French. It was Canada that was "petitioner." The Prime Minister agreed, but was more interested in an official visit to France in 1971, such as had been hinted at by Schumann. As previously mentioned, Schumann reacted with embarassment to an attempt to pursue this matter, and it became evident that Trudeau was still not welcome in Paris.

Looking back, it is all too clear that while it was easy to talk of specific projects to improve the substance of our relations, there were few of such projects on hand and not much interest among ministers. Despite a personal letter from Mitchell Sharp to his colleagues explaining the reasons for the policy and encouraging their cooperation, there was little reaction. Léo Cadieux made the rounds of some of his former colleagues and the way these conversations went explains the meagreness of the results. He ended up dealing more with symbols than with substance.[1]

His first visit for this purpose was in an area which depended on Canadian domestic policy rather than on cooperation from the French.

Canada had a large and expensive Immigration Office in Paris, 70 percent of whose clients were not French-speaking. The question was: how to concentrate more effort on the elusive French, who generally were not emigrants but who might be induced to consider emigration by a favourable presentation of the state of the Canadian economy? Would the Minister of Immigration come to see for himself? He would if he could apparently, but he did not. It was only after continuing pressure from the Embassy and the Quebec government and negotiations with the province that some years later Quebec immigration officials were attached to Canadian immigration offices and a steady trickle of French-speaking emigrants to Canada began.

For the Minister of Industry and Commerce the problem was the perennial one of how to raise the volume of trade between two countries who were amongst the leading trading countries in the world above the static figure of 1 percent of the total. The French were only interested in our primary products, while we wished to sell them more manufactured goods to offset the regular import from France of luxury articles. The Franco-Canadian Mixed Economic Commission was to meet in the spring, and the Ambassador asked whether there would there be specific projects from the Canadian side? Wait and see! He suggested that French economic journalists should be invited to Canada, sectorial missions mounted and Franco-Canadian industrial cooperation in small and medium-sized business encouraged. Canadian and French ministers should discuss these and other possibilities. Since the officials of the Canadian Industry and Commerce Department were not focused on Europe, nor was the Canadian business community, we did not expect much action.

Cadieux next visited his successor at National Defence; the unilingual Canadian Chief of Staff had just paid a friendly visit to his French opposite number. The Ambassador and the Minister reviewed the current small but successful officer exchange programs and reached agreement on a naval visit to France by HMCS *Ottawa*, the first Canadian bilingual naval vessel. A visit to the Secretary of State produced a Canadian contribution to the new organ in the Cathedral of the town of St. Malo, from where Jacques Cartier had sailed on his voyages to Canada. Both these projects improved the Canadian presence in France but hardly added substance to our relationship.

It is instructive to look at a similar visit made by Ambassador Cadieux three years later. While relations were by then normal and visits in both directions had greatly increased, there had been little progress with new substantive projects except in the scientific area, where there was considerable professional contact and a joint project to build a telescope in Hawaii seemed likely to proceed. Trade had not increased, though Canada's search for a relationship with the European Community was the cause of difficult but regular discussions (see Chapter 20). Immigration from France had regressed; the Minister never did come to Paris although his Quebec opposite number did.

The Ambassador's first visit to Quebec was useful and informative. Premier Bourassa had just gone through the October Crisis and was turning his mind to his first interest and priority, the economic future of the province. He was due to pay an official visit to France in April 1971, the first since that of Daniel Johnson in 1966, and he made it clear to the official responsible for the trip that he would not tolerate the sort of incidents that had marred the Johnson visit, when the Canadian Ambassador was not present at official functions. He was fed up with the "protocol nonsense," and if the Canadian Ambassador was not invited to the Elysée he himself would not go. He also wanted cooperation between the Embassy and the Quebec Delegation. He had heard a great deal about French investment in Quebec from De Lipkowski but had yet to see any. His primary purpose in going to Paris was economic, and he would judge the success of his visit by the extent of discussions on economic and investment matters. If France wanted to help Quebec it was in that area it could do so.

This was very refreshing, but during lunch with the Quebec officals the Ambassador was reminded that the problem of agreement within Canada was far from resolved. His hosts were Claude Morin, Yves Michaud, the newly appointed Commissioner for Foreign Cooperation, and some of their colleagues. From them he heard a different, though familiar, argument in which form was still more important than content because it could lead to a Quebec international personality: "Only Quebec could speak with authority internationally on Francophone matters, it was unacceptable that Anglophone provinces such as Ontario and New Brunswick, even with Francophone minorities, should participate in international Francophone conferences on the same basis as Quebec. That they should do so was clearly an Ottawa plan to surround Quebec." Ambassador Cadieux replied that no one contested the preponderant interest that Quebec had in La Francophonie, but the federal policy of bilingualism and biculturalism applied to the whole country, and was designed to enable the Francophone minorities outside Quebec to enhance their ability to maintain French education and culture by participating in this policy at national and international levels. The riposte of Michaud was that he believed that there was a diversity of sovereignty between the different members of a federal state for matters within their own competence. He preferred to speak of "member states" within the Canadian Federation rather than "provinces." None of this was new, it was in fact depressingly familiar. Morin had been presenting the same advice to Gérin-Lajoie of the previous Liberal government six years previously.

Cadieux also visited Ontario where he found, as in Quebec, considerable unhappiness with the federal government's dealings with the provinces on La Francophonie. Whereas in Quebec the complaints were related to a fundamental difference of interpretation of the Canadian constitution, in Toronto they reflected an unwillingness on the part of Ottawa to consult or inform until the last minute, and a tendency to take Ontario for granted. Ottawa had yet to learn that if it was to present a common front within La Francophonie, preoccupation with the byzantine negotiations with Quebec should not be at the expense of its natural allies in the other provinces. [2]

As normalization of Franco-Canadian relations slowly started to take effect, it was inevitable that there would be a reaction from those in Paris and Quebec who yearned for the Gaullist days of exclusive relations between Quebec and Paris. It took three forms. First, those connected with the forthcoming visit of Bourassa to Paris tried to arrange a visit similar to those of Johnson or Cardinal. There was to be much *éclat* and many symbolic meetings highlighting Quebec's independent status, but little substance. These plans were generated in part by the Quebec Delegation, which disliked finding itself no longer the sole repository of French interest in Canada. Its position began to revert to one more appropriate to a provincial delegation, while the Canadian Embassy, freed from the Gaullist embargo and under an active new Ambassador, started to rediscover its traditional role vis-à-vis the French government. If Premier Bourassa wanted to achieve his economic goals then the program for his visit would require considerable change. Word was passed to him, and his own office took over the arrangements for the visit under his personal supervision. The second reaction was the spreading of a rumour in Paris that became current in official as well as unofficial circles, that Canada's normalization of relations with France would prevent Quebec from carrying out its policies under its Education and Cultural Agreements with France. This was nonsense but considerable time was spent scotching the rumour, which had reached the ears of Maurice Schumann. Mitchell Sharp made it very clear in his next meeting with Schumann that there had been no change in the operation of Quebec's agreements or in Canada's positive attitude toward these agreements. Finally the trouble-makers in Quebec and Paris tried to create a new crisis in Franco-Canadian relations on the occasion of the next Conference of Francophone Ministers of Education.

In this atmosphere it seemed the time had come to go to the Elysée and review matters with Raimond, President Pompidou's Foreign Affairs Counsellor. Fortunately, my friend André Bissonnette, an Assistant Under-secretary of State in External Affairs, was in town for a meeting of the Agence Francophone, so we used the occasion to call on Raimond. Bissonnette had already been told by one of Raimond's colleagues that President Pompidou had no doubt that the solution of the Canadian problem was in national unity. He could not express this view in public because of the political strength of the ultra-Gaullists amongst his supporters. This official, however, went on to say that despite the improvement in relations, the attitude of Prime Minister Trudeau to such improvement was an unknown quantity and that he should make a gesture to clarify his position.

When we saw Raimond early in February 1971, I was able to dispose of the so-called doubts about Trudeau's attitude to improved relations between the two countries, by outlining the various steps Canada had taken in the past year to improve relations; these had culminated in Trudeau's appointment of a senior member of his own Cabinet as the new Ambassador to France, and the introduction of this colleague by way of a personal letter to President Pompidou. In addition, there would be important occasions in the coming year to improve relations still further, such as the meeting of the Mixed Economic Commission and the visit of the French Minister of Foreign Affairs in the autumn. Raimond's response was to the effect that recent events had removed an ambiguity with regard to French policy toward Canada, and that the French government had no intention of interfering in our internal affairs and hoped to avoid any artificial incidents. Better relations with Canada, however, must not be established at the expense of the special relationship between France and Quebec. Bissonnette's conclusion from the conversation was that the present state of our relations was satisfactory and improving. I agreed, but pointed out that there were limits to any rapid improvement. The abandonment of the Gaullist attitude toward Quebec and Canada could only be slow as long as there continued to be resistance in some circles of the French government and its civil service.

If we needed proof of this resistance it was provided forthwith, during arrangements leading up to the next Meeting of the Francophone Ministers of Education, due to be held in Paris. Jurgensen and his Quebec friends used the occasion to try once again to achieve international status for Quebec. They knew that they could no longer get away with a direct invitation to Quebec, as they had in Gabon. This time they sent two invitations via the French Ambassador in Ottawa, the first to the Canadian government, also asking it to inform the partially Francophone provinces, the second to the Quebec government as a "participating government" in La Francophonie. Ottawa was asked to pass on this second invitation. If it accepted this procedure Ottawa would be giving the green light for any foreign government that wished to invite a Canadian province, for whatever reason, to an international event attended by other sovereign states. The federal government's right to be considered the only interlocutor for communication to and from foreign governments would disappear as Quebec, and other provinces as well, could insist on exercising their right to communicate internationally on matters within their jurisdiction.[3]

This attempt to awaken old controversies was particularly unacceptable in that the procedure established between Ottawa and the provinces had worked satisfactorily for the last two years, and in this case the Quebec Minister of Education had already been named to lead the Canadian delegation while other provinces had been informed of the Conference. It would be tiresome to repeat here the same old arguments that had to be made to the French once again as to why their latest ploy was unacceptable. Suffice it to say that Ottawa effectively accepted the first invitation as having been issued to all of Canada including Quebec, and returned the separate invitation to the French Ambassador. In taking this approach it consulted with Quebec ministers as to how to proceed. When Mitchell Sharp saw Maurice Schumann the following month, the French Minister claimed he had permitted the letters to go forward in good faith since he had been advised by his civil servants that the approach taken was satisfactory to the Canadian government. Sharp explained why this was not so, and there the matter rested. This incident indicated that despite "normalization," we would still have to be on the alert for further attempts to give Quebec international status.

It was at this time, on April 15, 1971 that I departed from Paris, once again leaving my family behind me to follow after school was over, in order to take up a new appointment in Ottawa as the first Director General of the Bureau of European Affairs. I was fortunate to be leaving at a time when relations between France and Canada were on the mend, and as proof of this the large Canadian press group began to dissipate the same year. There is seldom press interest when things go well. It had been a difficult three and-a-half years for my family, and a period in which I had learned the meaning of the word stress. My new appointment involved all of Europe and included heavy managerial responsibilities. However, I would still be concerned with Franco-Canadian relations, this time from the Ottawa end.

Meanwhile, Bourassa's visit to Paris went ahead and from the Quebec and the Canadian points of view, was a considerable success. The Premier had declared before he left that he wished to create an atmosphere that would favour the development of French investment in Quebec and to deal with specific economic cases that had been awaiting resolution for a long time. This was language that the Pompidou government understood, and Bourassa was able to meet a widely representative group from the French business community and those ministers who dealt with French economic and technological policy. The Premier also made it clear in his public and private statements that his government believed in a federalist system. That his visit was successful was due to the fact that he and his entourage stuck to their economic objectives and were not diverted into the kind of symbolic gestures that had been *de rigueur* in the past. [4]

The Quebec clique that sought international status was furious at the Premier's remarks, believing, as they said, that Canada had no right or place when the interests of France and Quebec were being discussed. These "loyal" civil servants had no hesitation in attacking their Premier behind his back, claiming that, despite his intelligence and economic expertise, he was weak-willed and open to pressure from Ottawa. He did not have the imagination to understand that his political future depended on the constitutional question, and not on economic expansion and the fight against unemployment. There is a familiar contemporary ring to these complaints.

There were no unseemly protocol incidents during the visit. The Canadian Ambassador was invited by President Pompidou and his Foreign Minister to the appropriate ceremonies and meetings, and the Embassy was able to provide advice on the economic and trade side. The Canadian Minister-Counsellor had been a classmate of the Premier's at Law School. Bourassa's public speeches dealt with Quebec's unique place within North America and showed how the province should be seen as a factor enriching the Canadian federation. He used what was to become a familiar formula: "Quebec wished to conserve its cultural autonomy within a federalist system that worked."

During the lunch given by President Pompidou the Premier mentioned De Gaulle's visit in 1967 which, while it had certainly succeeded in mobilizing awareness of the problems of the French Canadians, had in the end done more harm than good, because De Gaulle had used the slogan of a separatist party and then taken an intransigeant attitude toward the rest of Canada. Pompidou replied that De Gaulle had been carried away by the enthusiasm of the moment, but what was important now was that De Gaulle was dead and a new president was directing the destinies of France.

Specific and concrete economic issues were on the agenda that Quebec could and would pursue, there had been no Federal-Quebec incidents, and the French government had conducted itself in accordance with the norms of international behaviour. Normalization had been taken a step further and France would be increasingly careful to ensure that its policies toward Canada would not place it in the position of having to choose between Ottawa and Quebec.

Two events in Ottawa during the remainder of 1971 are worth mentioning, not only because of their intrinsic importance for the continuing relationship, but also because no such events had taken place since De Gaulle's speech in Montreal in 1967.

The last meeting of the Franco-Canadian Mixed Economic Commission had been held four years previously, while the last journey of a French Foreign Minister to Ottawa dated even further back. The importance of a meeting between two of the world's leading traders was the opportunity it afforded to discuss international and bilateral questions at a key moment for Canada, when the United Kingdom was renegotiating its entry into the European Community, which would result in the disappearance of Commonwealth preferences. Canada would have to establish some form of relationship with the European Community. This meeting provided a good example of the short-sightedness of De Gaulle's policy of minimum contact with the federal government, for it made little sense for two large trading countries to be unable to consult regularly, for reasons that had nothing to do with global economic trends or specific trade problems.

The importance of Maurice Schumann's 1971 visit to Canada was not the content of his talks with Canadian ministers but the fact that he came at all. The two Ministers responsible for foreign affairs had continued to meet twice a year at NATO and the UN throughout the difficult De Gaulle years and after, for the purpose of discussing the bilateral relationship. It was the only regular ministerial contact between the two countries at that time. A look at the agenda of the 1971 meeting shows why it was necessary for both countries to maintain regular contacts on foreign

French Foreign Minister Maurice Schumann (right) visits Ottawa, September 1971. He is accompanied by External Affairs Minister Mitchell Sharp (left), and Léo Cadieux, Canadian Ambassador to France.

affairs that went well beyond the problems of the Ottawa-Quebec-Paris axis. For the Canadians, the priority was to explain to the French our pre-occupation with finding a new economic relationship with Europe, in light of the expected British entry into the European Economic Community, and recent unilateral actions by President Nixon in the monetary and trade fields. Other topics included the entry of China into the UN, a new UN Secretary General, the Conference on Security Cooperation in Europe, and relations with the Soviet Union, which Trudeau had visited in the spring and from where Premier Kosygin was expected to arrive in the next few weeks. There were the usual bilateral questions, not, for once, related to French interference in Canadian affairs, but rather to areas of substance, such as our now regular consultations on aid questions and a forthcoming meeting in Paris on science and technology.

The Schumann visit was a success in itself. He had a relaxed meeting with some Canadian ministers and saw the Prime Minister. He should not, after this meeting, have had any doubts about Trudeau's interest in Franco-Canadian relations. In answer to the Prime Minister's expressed concerns about the enlargement of the European Community, President Nixon's moves on financial policy, and the dangers for Canada of any polarization between the Community and the U.S., he offered many words of understanding and nothing else—but then, economics were not the strong point of either Schumann or Trudeau. There was mutual satisfaction at the improvement in bilateral relations and the first moves of the Agence Francophone.[5] At the end of the visit two events occurred to dampen enthusiasm and remind the federal government that the Pompidou regime, in spite of normalization, still intended to keep a certain distance from Ottawa and maintain its policy of duality toward Ottawa and Quebec.

On the same day that Schumann was in Ottawa and had just seen the Prime Minister, President Pompidou, answering a question at a press conference about a possible visit to France of the Canadian Prime Minister, replied: "I see nothing inconvenient in Trudeau coming to France some day and we shall certainly at one time or another invite him, but he, like us, is in a pre-electoral period and we would not wish to trouble him in the circumstances."[6] At his own press conference in Ottawa, Schumann, having to cope with these cold and hardly welcoming words from his President, tried to attenuate their effect by stating that "the French Government certainly wanted to officially invite the Canadian Prime Minister and the only problem was the date, which had to be convenient to both sides." He then continued his remarks to the effect that France's links with Quebec were not directed against Ottawa, and were not incompatible with good relations with Canada. Having delivered himself of these sentiments he then visited Quebec, not by flying from Ottawa to Quebec but by returning to New York and then going to Quebec, to make the point to his Gaullists back home that France still considered its relations with Quebec to be separate from those with Canada. And so, it was clear once again that Trudeau remained an object of dislike for the Gaullists and had not been forgiven for his public remarks during the various incidents between France and Canada in the past, particularly during the De Lipkowski visit, which had been personally approved by President Pompidou.

NOTES

1. Ottawa Telegram to Embassy Paris, GEU 35, January 16, 1971.
2. Internal Memorandum by European Division (GEU), January 11, 1971.
3. Memorandum to Secretary of State for External Affairs from the Undersecretary, May 3, 1971.
4. Embassy Paris Telegram to Ottawa, no. 1253, April 23, 1971.
5. External Affairs Telegram to Paris, GEO, 559, September 30, 1971.
6. Embassy Paris Telegram to Ottawa, no. 3512, September 23, 1971.

20

CANADA AND THE EUROPEAN COMMUNITY: A CANADIAN
PRIME MINISTER RETURNS TO PARIS

THE SUBSEQUENT COURSE of relations between Canada and France is an important thread in the larger account of the evolution of Canada's economic relations with Western Europe. In the early seventies, the broadening European Economic Community was a matter of increasing concern in Canada. The impending disappearance of Commonwealth preferences forced the federal government to consider the possibility of a new economic relationship with Britain and the members of the European Community. The events to be described in this chapter brought, once more, France's conflicting attitudes toward Canada into play, but eventually led to a new and more reasonable relationship between the two countries. This development must be seen against the background of Canada's political and defence relations with Western Europe.

Primarily for political reasons, Canada had supported efforts to create a new European community, in the first instance through economic integration, and to counter the self-destructive nationalist forces that had almost wiped out European civilization. But the potential effect of the European Common Market on Canadian trade only began to dawn on Canada when Britain first applied to join Europe; suddenly Commonwealth (or as they were previously called, Empire) trade preferences were at risk. Though De Gaulle vetoed this first application, it was clear that the United Kingdom would try again, and with the arrival of Pompidou in power, the question was once more on the agenda. As the process continued Canada received a second shock. In August 1971, President Nixon took unilateral action on import surcharges which, while directed primarily against the European Community and Japan, had a much more immediate effect on Canada, his country's largest trading partner. Trudeau's government was leaving its age of innocence behind. It suddenly found that Canada no longer had a "special trade relationship" with the United

States, and no relationship at all with the European Common Market, now taking on a new lease of life after the departure of De Gaulle.

The situation was not improved by Canada's actions in the defence sphere. In 1969 the government had decided to remove half of Canada's 10,000 troops from Western Europe and to replace their presence by an unconvincing pledge to help defend Norway and Denmark with troops based in Canada. The main reason given for this change of policy—coming not long after the Soviet invasion of Czechoslovakia—was that Western Europe could now more easily defend itself. It was a move that expressed an inherent reaction against the continent from which most Canadians had come and which had involved them in two World Wars. This isolationism had been revived by the Suez fiasco of 1956 and the more recent intervention by De Gaulle in Canadian affairs. The decision naturally angered our Allies, for it further weakened a collective defence system already coping with De Gaulle's departure from the NATO integrated command, and threatened by similar calls to bring the troops home issuing from the United States Congress. At the time, the European assessment of Canada's action was that we were moving to a more continentalist position, and that the October Crisis had been so serious that Canada's "national unity crisis" would completely absorb the attention of the federal government.

It was as a result of these events that the much misunderstood "Third Option" was published by Mitchell Sharp.[1] The options for Canadian trade policy, of which the government chose the third, were: 1) The status quo; 2) Free Trade with the U.S.; and 3) A global broadening of Canadian trade patterns. This last option was to be sought particularly through agreements with the rising economic powers, Japan and the European Common Market. Canada's dealings with the Common Market, which eventually led to the Framework Agreement of 1976, are well documented and have been the subject of a number of publications. The purpose of the present chapter is to describe France's role in this convoluted process. In Canada, it was realized that France could halt easily any attempt to establish a relationship with the European Community. The chances that it would do so were high, given the state of our relations since 1967 and the French belief that we were a stalking horse for the Americans. Neither France nor the European Community had decided on how they should interact with the U.S. and Japan, and therefore any agreement with Canada could set a precedent for relations with both those countries.

To be successful Canada would have to convince the French that there was merit in an exploratory approach, without commitment by anyone. At this early stage, the French would be losing nothing by allowing the process to go forward until individual European members and the Commission in Brussels had heard our case. For some optimists in Ottawa, it was possible to envisage a day when we would have made sufficient progress with the Europeans for the Prime Minister to make a visit to all members of the Community to explain Canada's actions at the highest level, and to ask for assistance in ensuring that substantive negotiations could begin for a Canadian-European entente. He would in this process be told—and some of us believed this was essential to the maintenance of Canada's position in the Western Alliance—that if he wanted help from his European colleagues, there must be an end to policies that called into question the North American security commitment to Western Europe. If such a series of visits could be arranged then the first step should be to go to Paris, not only because the French would be the most difficult to persuade about our European objectives, but also because no Canadian prime minister had visited Paris since 1964. If there were successful discussions on a subject of wider international import than the perennial problems posed by the Ottawa-Quebec-Paris triangle, then we should be in a position to bring French interventions in Canada's internal affairs to an end.

The federal government first had to resolve a number of conundrums: What did it really want and expect from Europe? How should it start the approach? How could it convince the French to allow the process to go ahead? Canadian ministers had been explaining to their European colleagues for some time that Canada was concerned at being left in limbo between the U.S. and Europe where international trade was involved. Once the Community was enlarged, our important trade with the United Kingdom would suffer because of diminished access to larger European markets. Moreover, the European Community was emerging from the deep freeze imposed on it by De Gaulle's nationalist policies, and was beginning to look outward, with particular attention to the problems posed by the entry of Great Britain, Denmark and Ireland.

In Ottawa it was decided that, as a first step, a group of senior officials should visit Europe to explain why we believed that a closer medium- and long-term relationship with the new and enlarged Europe, the European Commission in Brussels and the individual member states, was required. Emphasis would be placed on the medium term rather than the immediate situation, in order to clarify the difference between the Canadian approach and that of the U.S., which wanted a formal relationship so that it could bring regular pressure to bear on specific problems. Canada was more interested in a relationship permitting our ties with Europe to grow as Europe itself evolved. The delegation, of which I was a member, left on a fishing expedition in June 1972, to see whether and how our relations with the Community could progress, and what the main stumbling blocks were.

We went to France first and encountered the expected difficulties. I saw my old contact at the Elysée, Saint-Légier, now replacing Jurgensen as Head of the North American Department, and explained the political reasons behind our visit. He was aware of them, but warned me that he had consulted his economic colleagues and did not see how France could favour a Canadian consultative mechanism with the European Economic Community, as it would be used by the Americans as a pretext to create one of their own. I explained that at this point we did not have any preconceived ideas about form or substance. What we hoped to achieve was the commencement of a dialogue for the medium term, covering a number of sectors such as energy, national resources and conditions of access, where the interests of Canada and Europe were complementary. Saint-Légier still thought we should concentrate on bilateral consultation with individual members of the Community; I replied that we already had and would continue to do so, but as foreign trade and probably other areas would become increasingly a Commission responsibility, we would want to be able to talk to Brussels as well. He was sympathetic and promised to plead our case with the "economists." [2]

To those hard-nosed gentlemen we made it clear that our approach involved no preconceived ideas on mechanism, but was linked rather to geopolitical considerations toward finding some balance in our overall relationship with the U.S., and dealing with certain questions that were outside normal trade consultations, such as dispute settlement, intellectual property and long-term supply of raw materials. The latter topic was a bait for the French, whom we knew to be interested. The French economists started to show more appreciation of our approach, which they termed serious, but clearly indicated that they would resist any kind of institutional arrangement with the Community at that time. [3]

The French Economic Director at the Foreign Ministry, Jean Brunet, specifically acknowledged in his toast at the official lunch that Canada was in a special position with regard to an enlarged European Community, that interesting ideas had been advanced and that the French were prepared to examine them. [4] This meant that for the moment, the French would allow us to proceed with our initiative, but we had little doubt that they would continue to resist any institutionalization of relationships because of the U.S.; indeed, they soon placed a formal objection in the Community's Council of Ministers against any form of institutional relations between the Community and industrialized third countries.

The Canadian mission's visits to the other members of the Community and the European Commission were more encouraging, and the next challenge was to get a specific item on Canada-Community Relations on to the formal EEC agenda. There was to be a meeting of the European Heads of Government in the autumn of 1972, which would mention the intention to continue discussions with the U.S. and Japan. Could we get Canada added to the list? Instructions were sent to our diplomatic missions to press the Canadian case and, thanks to the Federal Republic of Germany, where the Canadian exploratory group had been warmly received, and to our local Ambassador, the late Bill Crean, who had close contacts with senior German government leaders, it was suggested that Canada be specifically mentioned in the Heads of Government Communiqué as follows: "There should be increasing dialogue with Europe's industrialized partners, in particular the U.S., Japan and Canada." We now had a formal agreement to discuss what our future arrangements might be with the European Commission in Brussels. The French had at least allowed the dialogue to go forward, while the support of the Germans had been intended, in part, to bind Canada closer to Europe, so that there would be no further removals of Canadian troops from Germany. We had no doubt that when Trudeau next met the German Chancellor he would receive such a message.

The following year, 1973, saw slow progress, though our talks with the European Commission continued and separate diplomatic missions were opened in Ottawa and Brussels. There were many hindrances: France's concern about maintaining control over the Community's policies toward the outside world; uncertainty within the Community about relations with its industrialized partners; and the decision of the Nixon administration to put pressure on their European allies to maintain their links with the U.S., using for this purpose a "Year of Europe" in which, within NATO and with the European Economic Community, there should be dialogue leading to solemn declarations regarding the future of the transatlantic relationship. Canada was not consulted.

At this time an extraneous issue arose that worsened Franco-Canadian relations: the McTaggart Affair. David McTaggart was, and is, a member of the Greenpeace Foundation and was captain of one of their ships present during French nuclear tests at proving grounds in the South Pacific. After repeated warnings, McTaggart's ship was rammed by a French naval vessel and he was injured, particularly in one eye. He demanded compensation for damages and Canadian government support, on grounds that Canada had a policy against nuclear testing which it regularly expressed in the United Nations. The Canadian government considered that it had to support the claim because it had indeed taken such a position in the United Nations. The French reacted violently, charging that Canada was interfering in the basic elements of French national security policy, namely the maintenance of the French nuclear *"force de frappe,"* and was pursuing a policy to this effect in the UN. There is no need to follow this matter further; it was resolved in McTaggart's favour by an out-of-court settlement some years later. Its immediate effect was to provide ammunition for those in the Pompidou administration who did not wish for any further progress in Franco-Canadian relations or were suspicious of the Canadian approach toward the European Economic Community. Maurice Schumann was no longer the French Foreign Minister. He had been replaced by Michel Jobert, a stiff-necked Gaullist with presidential ambitions, who used the McTaggart affair as a pretext for cancelling a planned visit to Canada. Our Ambassador in Paris no longer had the easy *entrée* to the Foreign Minister that he had enjoyed in the days of Maurice Schumann.

The "Year of Europe" caused even further delays to the Canadian initiative. This American ploy was definitely unpopular with the Europeans, particularly the Community countries, which could not agree among themselves on their future relationship with the United States. They did not believe that formal declarations which, after negotiation, would contain the lowest common denominator of agreement, were likely to improve transatlantic relations. The whole idea was based on "linkages," very fashionable in Washington at the time, and envisaged tying together the security, economic and trade areas, all of which involved bilateral relations, NATO interactions and some form of agreement on future relations with the EEC. The whole matter became bogged down in issues of process rather than of substance. Canada, which had not been consulted, had to indicate to the Americans and Europeans not only its skepticism but its insistence on being part of the process.

During the "Year of Europe" the French made an unexpected suggestion on Canada's relations with the European Community. In the course of the usual ministerial consultations at the UN, Mitchell Sharp explained to Jobert Canada's difficult situation. The U.S., our major trading partner, was unilaterally discussing the possibility of making declarations for the future, jointly with the Community, which had nevertheless agreed in principle to discuss its future relationship with Canada. Jobert's reply that perhaps the best solution would be a separate declaration, to be agreed upon between Canada and the Community. Sharp remarked that similar proposals had been rejected in the past because of disagreement in principle on the institutionalization of consultation and the fear of setting a precedent for relations with the U.S. He did not have to point out that it was the French who were responsible for this refusal.[5]

In External Affairs we persistently returned to the question during the year, insisting with our European colleagues that they could not issue a declaration on the future of relations with the Americans without taking Canada into consideration, which in any case they had promised they would do. This persistence finally produced results when the Community responded officially and positively in November 1973, by asking Canada to state formally its views on the matter. We understood that in agreeing to this, France retained its objection in principle to institutionalized relations with industrialized third countries.

This step was encouraging. Work commenced on a Canadian reply and plans were undertaken for a possible series of visits by the Prime Minister to the nine members of the Community in 1974. But after the McTaggart affair, would the French receive Trudeau, whom the Pompidou administration had clearly been unwilling to invite in the past? Ambassador Cadieux made unofficial soundings to find out whether Jobert's suggestion regarding Canada's relations with the Community, followed by the Community's invitation to Canada to express its views, implied that at the appropriate time, a visit by Prime Minister Trudeau to explain the Canadian position. The initiative would naturally include a visit to France. The reply from Jobert's office was that this was a correct interpretation of events.

I still had my doubts, and when I called on Saint-Légier at the end of the year I was treated to a long disquisition on the importance of nuclear testing to France; there was an implied linkage between a settlement of the McTaggart question and France's attitude to the Canadian initiative regarding the Community. After my visit we received a formal note in reply to the Ambassador's informal probings about a prime ministerial visit which could also be interpreted as linking McTaggart to Canada's relations with the Community. The note had a long paragraph on the need for Canada to understand that nuclear tests were connected to the basic elements of French national security policy. This response came very close to blackmail, or it could be interpreted as such by some members of the Canadian government. It was decided to restrict this particular exchange to a limited group while we got on with the Canadian reply to the Europeans and tried to reach a settlement of the McTaggart case.

And then the unexpected happened: President Pompidou suddenly died of cancer in March 1974. The Prime Minister attended the funeral, as did Premier Bourassa; there were no incidents and Trudeau saw unofficially a wide spectrum of senior figures in the French press. The new French President, Valéry Giscard D'Estaing, was not a traditional Gaullist, though he had served as Minister of Finance during the Pompidou regime. Politically he was of the centre-right, but had his own movement and did not entirely depend on the ultra-Gaullists, though his Prime Minister, Jacques Chirac, was a Gaullist. We had no doubt that the French bureaucracy would continue to advise against support for the Canadian initiative in Europe and therefore a visit by the Prime Minister became all the more important, for he would have to convince the new President of the Canadian case.

The next step was the Canadian government reply to the European Community members and the European Commission, which was delivered in April. The Europeans replied in June, stating that they would study the reply. It was high time for the Prime Minister to visit all nine members of the Community and the Commission in Brussels, to obtain their support for the start of formal negotiations for a new relationship between Canada and the Community. First the Paris hurdle had to be overcome. President Giscard D'Estaing approved a visit for October, after which the Prime Minister would visit Belgium and the European Commission. His visits to the other members would take place in early 1975.

We still had doubts about the success of the meetings with the French. We continued to receive messages at the civil service level which were full of comprehension of our objectives but expressed doubts about matters of form and the competence of the Commission to negotiate with a country such as Canada. It would be easier to achieve Canadian objectives if Canada were to negotiate bilaterally with member states. We replied to these, explaining once again that since the new Europe was two-headed, with some matters falling under Commission jurisdiction and others within the competence of member states, and since the stated goal of the Community was to expand the range of matters under Community

Prime Minister Pierre Trudeau meets with President Valéry Giscard d'Estaing of France at the Elysée Palace, October 21, 1974.

jurisdiction, Canada was interested in an arrangement that would permit its relations with Europe to grow as Europe itself grew. We would wish to be able to talk to the Commission on matters for which it was responsible while continuing, as in the past, to speak with Community members on bilateral matters. Communications from the French civil service continued up to the arrival of the Prime Minister in Paris, so we had little doubt about the advice the French President would be receiving. The talks between Giscard and Trudeau would be the key to the success of both the visit and the Canadian European initiative.

The recent past was in the minds of all who accompanied Trudeau, together with an awareness that the relationship between the Canadian Prime Minister and the new President would depend upon how Trudeau put across the Canadian case on approaches to the Community. Giscard had wide economic experience; Trudeau did not. If the French President decided that the Canadian approach was not in France's interests he could stop the process. This would not only slam the door on Canada's access to the European Community but would also ensure that our bilateral relations returned to a state of cautious suspicion, until such time as the next "nationalist" government in Quebec would be tempted to ask for renewed French assistance in achieving its domestic agenda.

The Prime Minister's entourage were concerned that he was not yet intellectually engaged in the Canadian approach to the European Community, and did not fully understand the economic reasons driving it. Yet it was on the strength of the economic aspect of the Canadian case that Giscard was likely to decide whether to allow Canada to continue its European policy. Only one briefing had occurred before we left for the Canadian Base at Lahr in Germany, where we would rest and brief the Prime Minister before continuing on to Paris. The reader may imagine our reaction on learning that Mr. and Mrs. Trudeau planned to go skiing in the Alps for the weekend. Fortunately, an enormous blizzard grounded all flying in the mountains, so the Prime Minister got his briefing after all. It was on this occasion that he began to take an interest in what Canada might achieve in cooperation with a developing European Community, and in the link between this objective and the effort to inaugurate a more constructive era in our bilateral relations with France.

I remember with pleasure our arrival in Paris as the Canadian and French flags fluttered and *O Canada* was played. There were two civil servants in the back of the line (John Halstead and myself) who smiled contentedly at each other. We had been in the trenches for many years, facing the French both in Paris and in Ottawa, and it is rarely given to a diplomat to see an objective on which he has been working for years come to fruition while he is still on the job to enjoy it. Yet here was Trudeau in Paris, not for skiing, not for a funeral, but as the Head of our government on an important mission for Canada that only the federal Prime Minister could carry out. It had taken him six-and-a-half years and three elections to be invited to the capital of one of our "mother" countries.

What did the visit accomplish? Since the two men met alone it was difficult to sense the chemistry between them and we heard a variety of versions from those with special axes to grind. From the warmth of the President's reception and the careful hearing he gave to the Prime Minister, and the cautious satisfaction expressed by the latter, it seemed clear that the French would do nothing at this stage to complicate visits to the other members of the Community. That the President still had doubts is perhaps not surprising: for example, during the official dinner he sent Bernard Destremau (his Secretary of State for Foreign Affairs, who had replaced De Lipkowski) to see me, since we had served together in Brussels. I was asked to repeat the Canadian case for a relationship with the European Community, and to give my old colleague assurances that our initiative was serious and would be carried through to a conclusion, provided all Community members agreed.

The best indication of the success of this part of the visit is Giscard's behaviour during two crucial periods in the subsequent negotiations. The following year, when all European heads of government were asked to approve the opening of negotiations with Canada on a possible contractual link, the French President, despite advice to the contrary from his officials, raised the French objection in principle to formal links with other industrialized countries. He allowed the negotiations to go forward. When, in 1976, the contractual link had been negotiated, he again, in spite of his officials, approved.

The bilateral aspects of the visit were dealt with in meetings between the Prime Minister and his delegation and the French Prime Minister, Jacques Chirac, and a number of French ministers. Chirac was and is a convinced Gaullist, but above all a man of action. Many issues were discussed. Chirac made it clear that his government wanted to see tangible results from cooperation with all of Canada, and a number of ministerial visits in both directions were planned. At his luncheon following these meetings, attended by a large contingent of French ministers and other notables from the political, economic and journalistic spheres, Trudeau gave an impressive address, reflecting on the Ottawa-Quebec-Paris triangle. He stressed to the French the need to understand that a federal state involved a division of powers and that the Canadian federal government was entirely content that relations between France and Quebec, should flourish so long as they were kept within the limits prescribed by the Canadian constitution. His audience seemed to appreciate his words, coming as they did from someone who was a constitutional expert and politician whose intellect was engaged by the problem, but also from a Canadian and a Quebecer with an emotional commitment to its solution. He believed that after his talk the French understood his message—a view reflecting his reaction to the warmth of his reception rather than to any mass conversion of his audience.[6]

My account of direct French intervention in Canada ends here. From 1974 onward there were disputes over such matters as the continental shelf and fish, but in general France kept to its policy of non-interference and non-indifference, even when the Parti Québécois was in power in Quebec. This did not mean that there was no support for the Quebec separatist cause in France, or that France would in the future refrain from supporting Quebec separation. It did mean that from 1974 until the time of writing, French intervention was not an important element in Canada's constitutional disputes. If blame is to be laid for the the various constitutional impasses that have brought Canada to its present position, it must be laid upon Canadians themselves and their elected representatives.

NOTES

1. *International Perspectives*, October 1972.
2. Embassy Paris Telegram to Ottawa, no. 2072, June 20, 1972.
3. Embassy Paris Telegrams to Ottawa, nos. 2039 and 2040, June 16, 1972.
4. Embassy Paris Telegram to Ottawa, no. 2206, June 28, 1972.
5. Can. Del. New York Telegram to Ottawa, no. 1389, September 25, 1973.
6. Personal Letter, Taylor (Minister Canadian Embassy Paris)-Black, November 6, 1974.

ENVOI

IF CANADA is to remain as presently constituted with Quebec as one of its principal provinces, then the French Fact will continue to be part of the Canadian political scene and part of how Canada conducts its international affairs. Depending on whether a Canadian is raised and educated as a Francophone or Anglophone, he or she will react differently from fellow citizens brought up in the other tradition and respond differently to situations, be they political, cultural, emotional involving the two different cultures. If French-speaking Canadians are to feel identified with Canada's external policies and to play a part in formulating them, they must have a window on the world.

This means that Canada will continue to have a close and special relationship with France and the Francophone world, and within that relationship France will have programs in specific areas compatible with the Canadian constitution, with Quebec, and to a lesser extent with other partially French-speaking provinces. This relationship was recognized in the period 1967-1974, but will always require careful handling by the federal government if the rest of Canada is to understand, if not always approve, the legitimate requirements of Canada's largest minority. A special relationship with France is without doubt in Canada's national interest.

The reverse is not true. France is a major European power with wide interests in the future of the European Union, European security problems, the Middle East and the African subcontinent. The French remain suspicious of North America and particularly the U.S. because of its economic strength and the "Americanization" of French language and culture. The "cousins in Canada" are not high on the French agenda except in emotional terms; history and a bad conscience over leaving French Canada in the lurch more than two hundred years ago are compelling forces. Hence the willingness to assist in strengthening the French language and culture in Canada. But when it comes to economic matters, "the cousins" live in North American and are part of the NAFTA. As far as the French are concerned, Quebec will have to face the consequences of its geography and neighbouring economies essentially alone.

In this complex relationship disputes with France will inevitably erupt from time to time. It will be necessary for Canadian governments to differentiate between issues that are absolutely essential to Canadian interests and those problems that, while difficult, are in the nature of policy disagreement but not absolutely vital to Canadian interests. This distinction is sometimes difficult to make because there is a tendency, particularly among Canadians still inclined to fight another Battle of the Plains of Abraham, to consider every dispute with France a major confrontation, or alternatively, to refuse to recognize that in key cases French policy directly affects Canadian national interests. The events recounted here were the result of a decision by a French President to interfere directly in the internal affairs of Canada, and the Canadian government had no alternative but to contest them so as to protect the legally and democratically constituted order that is the Canadian Federal State.

This problematic relationship will continue until such time as Quebec evolves from its present ambiguity to a relatively settled position within the Canadian Federation and the North American context. France should become less of a crutch and more a source of inspiration helping to define and protect the French Fact on its own terms, not those of an out-of-date ethnic nationalism. In addition, the old British-French rivalry is becoming increasingly irrelevant given the changing nature of Canadian society. The competition of two former colonial powers is part of our history but not a reason for political movements at the dawn of the twenty-first century.

There remains a risk that Quebec will leave the Canadian Federation. How is France likely to react to this event? The vast majority of French politicians, Gaullists included, have insisted that separation would mean the eventual disappearance of the French Fact in North America. Yet France's policy toward Canada retains enough duality that if Quebec, after a successful referendum, should ask for assistance in establishing an international personality through full diplomatic recognition, France would likely oblige. This is especially true since the current President has been an active Gaullist throughout his political career, and sees himself as an heir to De Gaulle. If French recognition of an independent Quebec should occur, it would be one of the rare occasions in French history when sentiment prevailed over *raison d'état*.

APPENDIX

MEMORANDUM FOR THE MINISTER:
RELATIONS WITH FRANCE

1. Apart from a short visit to the Chancery to inspect the decoration arrangements, I spent all of my days in Paris at the residence, engaged in conversations with Léger concerning various aspects of our relations with France and more particularly the instructions which you had approved prior to my departure. On this latter point especially the conversations were difficult but in the end we managed to reach agreement.

2. Léger's basic concern, which of course is justified, was that unless we were extremely careful General de Gaulle would be irritated and there could be a new crisis in our relations. There was no difference between Léger and I on the importance of this consideration.

3. On the other hand my chief purpose was to induce Léger to understand fully that it was not possible for the Canadian Government to remain idle while the French Government, in its relations with Quebec, was in effect treating Quebec as an independent state and depriving Ottawa of control over an important sector of foreign policy. There were bound to be questions in the House and very serious questioning in the country if the Federal Government appeared to be unwilling to assert its authority and to maintain the constitutional position.

4. In the end I think I was able to persuade Léger that our whole approach was not a negative one. On the contrary, we did not want to prevent the development of relations between France and Quebec, but our hope was that these relations would develop within the appropriate framework which would allow for something more to be added. The objective of the Federal Government was to involve in relations with France, in addition to Quebec, federal institutions and other provincial governments. Furthermore, Léger agreed that it might be possible to

encourage the French to proceed along the lines we suggested without formally repudiating anything they had done up to now.

5.   Much of our discussion focussed on the request in the instructions that we should be informed of the purpose and programme of French Ministers who might come to Canada. For a while Léger argued that some of these Ministers might be coming over without any very definite scheme in mind and that it might not be possible for them to tell us in advance what could be the outcome of their conversations in Quebec. I acknowledged that we should not expect the French to tell us more than they could. I stressed however that it was essentially a matter of good faith. What was essential was that, as their plans were developing, they should not leave Ottawa out. It was at that stage that we could indicate whether national dimensions could be given to projects which might be conceived of initially in provincial terms. This would make it possible for us to determine at the crucial time whether or not any useful purpose would be served through a visit to Ottawa. If France and Quebec were to discuss their schemes in isolation it was obvious that there would no need at all for French Ministers to come to Ottawa and their notice to us would be an empty formality.

6.   In the end Léger agreed to seek an interview with Alphand and his aim is to present our request for the advance notification as to the visits of French Ministers in the light of our positive approach to the problem of expanding relations between France on the one hand and the whole of Canada on the other.

7.   Léger was still convinced that General de Gaulle would not be persuaded of our arguments. He still foresaw a risk of a new crisis and his judgement, with which I agree, was that at best the French might never give us a formal reply to the various points we have put to them. We might have to be satisfied that our representations will merely have an inhibiting effect and that the number of provocative gestures made as a consequence be avoided. We both agreed that it was too much to hope that the French would acknowledge that they had done wrong and that they would behave in the future impeccably from our point of view. Léger thought that we should resign ourselves to the prospect that there are likely to be a few more accidents before General de Gaulle disappears from the scene.

8.   All told, although the conversation was difficult and at times some-what heated, there was, I believe, a meeting of minds as to what we intended to do and we both felt that the exchange had been extremely valuable. I acknowledged freely that Léger was rightly concerned about the attitude of the Elysée, but as you will recognize, I was no less forceful in urging him to recognize that we had to have in mind the constitutional and political requirements of the situation here.

M. Cadieux
November 11, 1967

BIBLIOGRAPHY

PRIMARY SOURCES

Department of Foreign Affairs and International Trade [DFAIT],
formerly Department of External Affairs
Departmental Records
*National Archives of Canada [NA]
#Departmental Records-Canada-France
Relations

Privy Council Office Ottawa [PCO]
#Cabinet Conclusions
#Privy Council Records

*Private Papers and Notes E.P. Black

* Indicated Records are restricted.
# Obtained under Access to Information Act.

SECONDARY SOURCES

Alexandre, Phillipe. *Le duel de Gaulle-Pompidou* (Paris: Grasset, 1970).
Aron, Raymond. *La revolution introuvable* (Paris: Fayard, 1968).
De Gaulle, Charles. *War Memoirs: Unity, 1944-1946* (London:
    Weidenfield and Nicolson, 1959).
———. *Mémoires d'espoir: Le Renouveau,* 1958-1963 (Paris: Plon, 1970).
De Menthon, Pierre. *Je Témoigne* (Paris: Plon, 1979).
English, John. *The Life of Lester Pearson,* 2 (Toronto: University of
    Toronto Press, 1992).
Granastein, J.L. *Canada 1957-1967* (Toronto: University of Toronto
    Press, 1986).
———, and Robert Bothwell. *Pirouette: Pierre Trudeau and Canadian
    Foreign Policy* (Toronto: University of Toronto Press, 1990).

Head, Ivan and Pierre Trudeau. *The Canadian Way* (Toronto: M&S, 1995).

Lescop, R. *Le Parti Québécois du Général De Gaulle* (Montreal: Boréal Express, 1981).

Morin, Claude. *L'Art de l'impossible: la diplomatie québécoise depuis 1960* (Montreal: Boréal Express, 1987).

Pearson, Lester B. *Mike: The Memoirs of the Right Honorable Lester B. Pearson*, 1 (Toronto: University of Toronto Press, 1972).

Pickersgill, J.W. *Mackenzie King Record*, 1 (Toronto: University of Toronto Press, 1960).

————. *Mackenzie King Record*, 2 (Toronto: University of Toronto Press, 1968).

Robinson, Basil, H. *Diefenbaker's World* (Toronto: University of Toronto Press, 1967).

Sharp, Mitchell. *Which Reminds Me* (Toronto: University of Toronto Press, 1994).

Thomson, Dale. *Vive le Québec libre* (Toronto: Denau, 1988).

Tournoux, J.R. *La Tragédie du Général* (Paris: Plon, 1967).

Trudeau, Pierre. *Federalism and the French Canadians* (Toronto: Macmillan, 1968).

Viansson-Ponté, Pierre. *Histoire de la République Gaullienne*, 2 (Paris: Fayard, 1970).

INDEX

A

Alphand, Hervé, 14, 16, 51, 79, 82, 144
Aron, Raymond, 42

B

Basdevant, Jean, 49
Beaudry, Jean-Paul, 77
Beaulieu, Paul, 73-75 [arrival in France], 105, 129, 162
De Beaumarchais, Jacques, 113, 144
Bedson, Derek, 50
Bennett, W.A.C., 63, 64
Bertrand, Jean-Jacques, 57, 73, 77, 79, 86, 90, 92-93, 124, 130, 135, 139, 141
De Bettencourt, André, 31, 32, 36
Billecocq, Pierre, 158
Bissonnette, André, 95, 173-74
Bongo, Albert, 30-31, 86
Bourassa, Robert, 151-52, 169, 171-72, 175-76, 186
Broussine, Georges, 51, 80
Brunet, Jean, 182

C

Cadieux, Léo, 157, 159-62, [arrival in France] 169-70, 176, 185
Cadieux, Marcel, 11, 14-16, 19, 35, 38, 55, 70, 75, 111
Caouette, Réal, 120
Cardinal, Jean-Guy, 31, 32, 37, 57-58, 77-83 [visit to Paris], 92, 172
Castro, Fidel, 35
Chaban-Delmas, Jacques, 102

Chapdelaine, Jean, 23, 44
Charles V. 45 [Note 1]
De Chateaubriand, René, 45 [Note 1], 96
Chevrier, Lionel, 34
Chirac, Jacques, 186, 189
Chouinard, Julien, 90, 139, 141
Chrétien, Jean, 10, 97
Comiti, Joseph, 113
Couve de Murville, Maurice, 20-21, 30, 34, 37, 45, 55-57, 74, 77, 93, 98, 107-08
Crean, G.G. [Bill], 183
Cross, James, 165

D

Debré, Michel, 24, 45, 58, 79, 92, 100-02, 131
Destremau, Bernard, 189
Diefenbaker, John, 5-6, 79
Diori, Hamani, 85, 88-91 [1st Niamey Conference], 133-38 [2nd Niamey Conference], 140-41
Dorin, Bernard, 92
Drapeau, Jean, 12
Drew, George, 63
Duplessis, Maurice, 2, 5

E

Edward VII, 3

F

Fanton, André, 131, 142, 157
Foccart, Jacques, 31, 102, 138
Fontaine, André, 131, 143

G

Garet, Pierre, 125, 139
De Gaulle, Charles, 1, 3, 5-7, 9, 11,
   17-21 [press conference], 23, 30-
   31, 34, 41-45 [Events of May],
   47, 49-52 [Rossillon affair], 55,
   61-62, 64-65, 67, 73-75, 77-83
   [Cardinal visit], 86, 92-93, 97-99
   [departure from power], 101, 106,
   108-09, 113-14, 122, 130, 139,
   154, 158, 161, 165, 167-68, 176,
   179-80, 182, 194
Gérin-Lajoie, Paul, 7
Giscard D'Estaing, Valéry, 144, 168,
   186-89 [Trudeau visit]
De Goumois, Michel, 135
Goyer, Jean-Pierre, 52
Grey, The Earl, 3
Gromyko, Andrei, 113

H

Halstead, John, 123, 125, 126 [Note
   10], 131 [Note 2], 188
Hamon, Léo, 144, 146
Houde, Camillien, 71

J

Jamieson, Don, 100
Jobert, Michel, 184-85
Johnson, Daniel, 7, 13, 19, 30, 35,
   44, 55, 61, 77, 86, 171-72
Joxe, Louis, 37
Jurgenson, Daniel, 24, 49, 78, 87-88,
   92, 95, 102, 106, 121-22, 125,
   137, 141, 144, 154, 174, 182

K

Kosygin, Alexei, 177

L

Lalonde, Marc, 37, 86, 90, 101
Laporte, Pierre, 164-65
Laurent, Pierre, 100-01, 120, 125
Léger, Gaby, 15, 98
Léger, Jean-Marc, 91, 133
Léger, Jules, 3, 11, 14-17, 20, 23, 25,
   31, 35-37 [Paris Education
   Conference], 51, 73, 98

L

Lesage, Jean, 5, 6, 7
Lévesque, René, 24, 165
De Lipkowski, Jean, 45, 52, 64, 66,
   92, 100, 102-03, 106, 108, 109-
   19 [visit to Canada], 124, 129-31,
   136-38, 140, 142, 144-45, 157,
   169, 176, 178, 189
Loiselle, Gilles, 68

M

Malaud, Phillipe, 159
Malreaux, André, 95
Marchand, Jean, 19
Martin, Médéric, 71
Martin, Paul, 14-16, 19-21, 30, 85, 90
Masse, Marcel, 57, 90-92, 111, 127,
   129-31 [visit to France], 135, 139
McTaggart, Captain David, 183-86
De Menthon, Pierre, 25-26, 58
Michaud, Yves, 171
Michener, Roland, 3
Michelet, Edmond, 144
Missoffe, Francois, 10
Moboutu, Joseph, 86
Morin, Claude, 7, 31, 77, 86, 90, 99,
   106, 134-35, 139, 171-72
Morin, Jean Marie, 86, 124

N

Nixon, Richard, 177, 179

P

Patry, André, 44
Pearson, Lester B., 6, 8, 14, 21, 30,
   35, 49, 100, 130
Pelletier, Gérard, 74, 90, 95-97, 129,
   139-41 [2nd Niamey Conference],
   158
Pepin, Jean-Luc, 32, 99
Peyrfitte, Alain, 10, 29, 48
Pleven, René, 107, 114
Poher, Alain, 102, 120, 140
Pompidou, Georges, 37-38, 43, 45,
   98-99, [Events of May] 102-03,
   112-13, 117, 120-21, 137-38,
   140, 144, 159, 162, 164, 173,
   175-76, 178-79, 186
Prefontaine, René, 50

R

Raimond, Jean Bernard, 107, 125,
    138, 173
Robarts, John, 169
Robichaud, Louis, 35, 48, 86-87
Roccard, Michel, 165
Rossillon, Phillipe, 47-52 [in Canada],
    89, 91, 106
Rothschild, Baroness, 95

S

Saint-Légier, René de la Saussaye, 25,
    41, 43-45 [Events of May], 58,
    82-83, 87, 107, 182, 185
St. Laurent, Louis, 15
Schumann, Maurice, 102, 105-06,
    109, 111, 113, 117, 121-24 [De
    Lipkowski visit], 127, 130, 136,
    139-40, 143, 145, 148, 151-53,
    158, 160, 163, 166, 169, 173-74,
    177-78 [visit to Ottawa], 184
Senghor, Léopold, 29
Servan-Schreiber, Jacques, 159
Sharp, Mitchell, 36, 58, 79, 81, 102,
    105-06, 109-19, 122-25 [De
    Lipkowski visit to Canada], 127,
    130-31, 143-48 [visit to Paris],
    151-53 [renewal of Cultural
    Agreement], 158, 162, 165, 167,
    169, 173-74, 180
Stalin, Joseph, 3
Stanfield, Robert, 19, 157

T

Taylor, J.H.[Si], 191 [Note 6]
Tremblay, Paul, 144
Trudeau, Pierre Elliot, 10, 19, 35, 37,
    47, 50-51, 55-57, 80, 85-86,
    89-90, 92-93, 102, 106-07, 112,
    115, 121, 124, 127-28, 135, 140,
    151, 164-65, 169, 173, 177-78,
    183, 185-89 [visit to Paris]

V

Valèry, Paul, 18
Vanier, Georges, 3

W

Windsor, Edward Duke of, 71

DATE DUE
